Breathe

*An Anthology Full of Inspirational Stories
Compiled by*

MELINDA WALKER

Breathe
An Anthology Compiled by Melinda Walker

Copyright © 2018 by Believe In Your Dreams Publishing
All rights reserved.

The reproduction, distribution, transmission, or utilization of this work in whole or in part in any form by any electronic, mechanical, or other means, including photocopying, recording, or any type of storage of information, is forbidden without written permission. For permission requests, please contact Melinda Walker and Nichole Peters at:

Believeinyourdreamsproductions@gmail.com

These works are based on actual events. In certain cases, incidents, characters, and timelines have been changed for dramatic purposes to protect the privacy of the individuals.

Acknowledgements

I would like to first thank my Heavenly Father for giving me this opportunity to be able to accomplish such an honorable goal in this life. I'm so grateful to him and I'll forever praise him. I also would like to thank Nichole Peters, my ride or die, my childhood friend whom I love dearly, and Believe In Your Dreams publishing company for affording me this GREAT opportunity and for doing such a GREAT job. Thank you from the bottom of my heart.

I want to thank my mother for raising me and providing for me, sometimes working three jobs as a single parent to assure that my sister and I were provided for. Thank you, Momma.

I dedicate this book to my spiritual mother, Barbara Jean Holloway. May she rest in heaven. The last conversation we had made me think about the song the William Brothers sing that says, "If I can't do nothing else, I just humble myself and I take this moment out just to say thank You, and if my life should end this day and not another blessing comes my way, all I need is one breath just to say thank You." She said this journey was a humbling experience, and she told me, if the Lord chose not to heal her, she still says thank You as she waved with that big hand that left an imprint on my life. Those hands laid a great anointing on my life, and I send a kiss and a thank you to heaven to her.

I acknowledge and thank my paternal grandmother for introducing me to the ways of God, for bringing me to church and building my foundation in God. I thank you, Momma (I called her Momma) in heaven. I thank my Pastor Jessie Holloway, who is my spiritual father and who has stood in the place of my beloved father, whom I miss dearly. Pastor Holloway introduced me to Jesus in a profound way. He taught me the Word and he walked before me in the Word. He dealt with those outstanding features in my life that would be a hindrance to my growth. I truly thank him for demonstrating true deliverance.

I thank my friend Tina Watts, whom I've had to *BREATHE* to for twenty-five years. She has ALWAYS been there for me. I love that woman. I'm thankful for my only sister, who is not only my sister but my friend. As adults, we have been nothing but sisters to one another. I thank you for being my big sis.

Last but not least, I'm thankful for my immediate family. To my children, Laura, Marquise, and Destiny: You have been through all the struggles with us, the ins and the outs, the ups and the downs. We made it through, and as a family, we are stronger, wiser, and better. I love you all and thank you for loving me as your mom. To my husband of twenty-five years as of March 28, Wilbert Walker: I definitely would not be where I am without you. I wouldn't have the testimony I have without you. We've been through it all—and I mean it *all*—but we still find a way to forgive and pick up the pieces and move forward. You are a good man who works hard to take care of your family. Despite it all, I love you and I say thank you. God caused it to work together for my good. Yes, He meant it for our good.

This has been a journey, and I'm thankful for everyone who is and has been a part of my journey. Simply, thank you.

BREATHE
An Anthology Compiled by Melinda Walker

On the behalf of Believe In Your Dreams Publishing, we would like to express an abundance of gratitude, love, and blessings to Melinda Walker. Thank you for trusting the Believe In Your Dreams Publishing and Production team with your amazing project. May your book rock the broken hearts of so many around this globe who need fresh air to **BREATHE** to heal their wounded souls.

Believe In Your Dreams Publishing would like to extend further appreciation to every co-author who shared their heartfelt true stories to the masses. I pray each story will touch and, hopefully, bring breakthrough to the lives of many people across this great nation. Thanks for *believing* in me and my rocking team. We love, adore, and appreciate you all.

~ **CEO, Nichole Peters**
Believe In Your Dreams Publishing

Table of Contents

	Page
Foreword: As Long As Life Lasts, BREATHE By Nichole Peters	1
I Took a Deep Breath and I Let It Go by Melinda Walker	9
Prescription for Survival: Blood of Faith in My Spiritual Veins by Sarah E. Anderson	17
Excess Baggage by: Rita Taylor	25
Once the Healing Began, I was Able to Breathe by: Arlene Walker	32
Stop, Drop & Quantum Leap Into Redemption and Your Destiny by: Derricka Holliman	38
When the Enemy Rushed in Like a Flood, I Decided to Exhale by: Schynies Williamson	43
Your Past is Necessary, Just *Breathe* by: Maritza Johnson	50
Many Are the Afflictions of the Righteous, But God by: Tina Watts	57
The Eyes of God by: Minister Niechie Baker	63

BREATHE
An Anthology Compiled by Melinda Walker

How God's C.P.R. Restored My Spiritual Pulse: The Resuscitation by: Gwendolyn Braswell Burkes	75
Surrendering in the Storms of Life by: Jennifer L. May	83
Overcoming the Impossible by God's Grace by: Demetre Francis	91

Foreword:
As Long As Life Lasts, BREATHE
By: Nichole Peters

"The Spirit of the God has made me. And the breath of the Almighty gives me life." Job 33:4

Hear ye . . . hear ye . . . to all the people from around this great nation. We bring to you one powerful message that can carry you abundantly for the rest of your life, a profound message to help you encounter, heal, forgive, release, exhale, and to just **BREATHE**.

I have so much gratitude and appreciation to do the Foreword in this anthology. There are not many authors around the world who grew up with each other and decided to collaborate on their stories to the world together. This is what Melinda Walker, the author and compiler of this book, and I share.

I will never forget the days when she and I used to go walking around Poplas Quarters. We didn't stay in the best neighborhood, but we made the best out of it. Some of us used to hurry up with homework so we could go to Mays grocery store to play video games. We use to put money in the jukebox and dance until the streetlights came on. Dancing was exciting and therapy for us even as children. We stayed at each other's houses many nights, still dancing.

The main thing I will never forget is the days I sat on the hot concrete steps in Redmond Heights Projects in the small town of Bogalusa, Louisiana, where I grew up at. I would sit there over an hour just dreaming and believing away. I told my grandmother, "Grandma, I am going to make it out this hood one day, and God is going to make sure I come get as many of my family and friends as I can to make sure they, too, will be great."

My grandmother replied, "Baby girl, God's got you set out for so much more; just watch and see. All I ask of you is, when the Good Lord reveals all of your gifts, Nikki Pooh, use them for the good that is in you and for others."

I sat there thinking with my young mind about what the Lord might have revealed to my grandma about me. I remembered how my heart was racing so fast, and I was breathing very hard and strong. That powerful feeling was a praise moment. I was so young I didn't even recognize I was so full of joy because of what Granny had just revealed to me through God. Granny used to prophesy over my life all the time. Always remember, iron sharpens iron. Proverbs 27:17 says, "As iron sharpens iron, so one man sharpens another."

As I got older, I went through so many defeats and raging storms. I realized God did have more for me, just like He has more for each us. Seeing me live out my dreams as an international bestselling author/publisher is a dream come true. I thank God for letting my childhood visions come to harvest. Now I am using my purpose to help my family, my ride or die, some of closet friends, and people I didn't even know, but who I knew had a powerful story to tell. There is power in speaking life into existence and there is power in walking straight into your destiny. I thank God for granting me the position for hundreds of women and men to get their work published so their stories too can help heal this hurting nation. This is what I consider winning with great success through God. Now when I *BREATHE*, it feels like a robust feeling of passion and perseverance. Paving the path for others to *BREATHE* by breaking chains is victory. Oh, yes, my set-free hands are raised up!

BREATHE
An Anthology Compiled by Melinda Walker

I pray that each reader learns from our pasts, our wrongdoings, our mistakes, our setbacks, our traumas, and our trials. I pray that you witness your triumph in our testimonies. I pray that you *BREATHE*, knowing that each breath you take is your gift of life each day that Father God grants you. Job 32:8 says, "But it is spirit of man, and the breath of the Almighty, that give them understanding." In each story, we are asking you to relax so you can encounter, understand, and enjoy your experience with Father God. You'll be able to relate what the love of God can do for all his children. This anthology was written to help bring healing power to the soul of the broken, oppressed, wounded, abused, depressed, and dry-boned.

We welcome you to many life experiences, so you can be able to respect life's breakthroughs. Each author will feed into your soul by sharing moments of their testimonies of trusting and relying on just Father God. Each author wants to you to raise your hands, touch your mindset, and comfort your hearts so you will be able to *BREATHE* again, even if we must take you back to how the Creator first had you take your first breath. "That He formed us (Man) all from dust from the ground, and breathed into man's nostrils the breath of life; and we (Man) became a living being" (Genesis 2:7).

Readers, let me share a little of my testimony with you. When I was a little child, I use to have horrible, demonic nightmares where some days I was afraid to sleep at night. I wore an outfit of hidden grief that I carried with me for years, and on top of it all, I was going through agonizing hurt, pain, and abuse from life. I was tired! It seemed like I was literally suffocating off all the dark smoke. I felt like nothing but hot air was scorching my soul. I was literally choking to death by letting the enemy come change my mindset.

BREATHE
An Anthology Compiled by Melinda Walker

Instead of me stopping to take a deep breath to pray and rebuke the enemy so he could flee, and believe with just a little faith of a mustard seed, I flipped out and did the total opposite.

Boy, did I get lost in the darkness and wilderness, and I became rebellious and adopted an attitude called wrong turn on life. I even decided to stop praying because I felt like Father God didn't love me either. I felt like a bucket of dry bones, like I was DOA! I felt like no one loved me but my Ma'dear. I was starting to think I was in the Book of Job, but my mindset and faith weren't as strong as my brother Job's were. He believed that Our Lord and Savior Jesus Christ was with him even though he suffered; but me? I believed He didn't want to save me, so why live? I was ready to die. You have no idea how many times the enemy tried to convince me to kill myself. I actually started believing this slick, slew-footed, no-good fool.

One of the biggest mistakes of my life was, instead of turning to God, I turned to more darkness, the vicious streets, and some of the things that came with it, especially after losing my father and grandmother months apart. They were two of the main leaders in my family, besides my amazing Ma'dear (my Mom), who always told me to never settle and go be great. My father used to tell me I was his chocolate princess. He always reminded me I would always be loved by him, and I was more than a conqueror. I was angry and bitter at God for taking them away from me. My grandmother and I lived together from the time I was born until the time she took her last breath. She was very wise and she was my hero.

My devastated soul felt so useless without them. I lived in secret grief for years about my granny and my father, even though my father had lived a double life. When this was revealed to me, I felt shame and anger toward him, but because of the love we shared for one another, my anger didn't last long. I forgave him and loved my father just like he loved his princess.

There I was in my early twenties, taking nitroglycerin heart pills, going in and out the hospital for my irregular heartbeat and genetic diabetes, stressing so bad I had to wear a heart monitor around my chest when they discharged me, deeply depressed. I felt lost without them. During my distress, I picked up on major bad habits and a couple of bad men too. I started hanging more with the wrong crowds. I felt more love in the streets than I did from some family members and friends.

I thought the man I feel deeply in love with would never put his family in jeopardy, but he did. I never knew he was a notorious drug dealer until it was too late. I had already fallen deeply in love with him. I thought I was one of the queens of the streets and had it all. But don't get it twisted: This lifestyle or any get-rich-scheme lifestyle can cause you more pain and abuse than any dollar bill you can bank on. Always remember that fast money is temporary money. Never lose your spirit of light over Mr. No-Good.

Dollar bill. Chasing that dollar bill and doing things out of the spirit of mammon (putting idols of money or any power over God) almost got me killed. Don't let it kill you. I will never forget how cold the steel from that pistol pointed at my forehead felt. I was also five months pregnant. If it wasn't for me being pregnant and God sparing my life, I would've been dead.

The evil maniac told me, "I would've blown your head off if it wasn't for you carrying that baby in your belly."

BREATHE
An Anthology Compiled by Melinda Walker

I remember being so shaken up that I literally had to go straight to the ER after that episode. I almost lost my mind, but my God had another master plan for his daughter. He awakened me, fed my soul, my heart, and mind with His major powerful antidotes of wisdom and understanding. I decided to do like my brother Job and trust God with everything the enemy was trying to snatch from me. At that very moment, I learned to *BREATHE* and PRAY like never before. I was so full of gratitude for the Lord's grace and mercy, especially for giving me another chance at LIFE! Thank You, Father God, for turning my life around and for letting me live out all my life's purposes, instead of destroying all my life's purposes. Am I perfect? Nope, but there is power in every breath we take. I've realized, like my brother Job, that the breath in my nostrils is more powerful than anything, and you must too. Job 27:3 says, "As long as life is in me, and the breath of God is in my nostrils."

Are you ready to *BREATHE* through the power of prayer and purpose? Shout now, my brothers and sisters. Are you ready to heal those dead or dry bones? Then He said to me, "Prophesy to the breath, prophesy, son of man, and say to the breath, 'Thus says the Lord GOD, Come from the four winds, O breath, and breathe on these slain, that they come to life.' So, I prophesied as He commanded me, and the breath came into them, and they came to life and stood on their feet, an exceedingly great army" (Ezekiel 37:9-10).

Are you ready to stand and raise your hands from any dead situation? Keep breathing! Put on your mighty warrior cape, knowing that Father God is big enough, that no weapons formed against you shall prosper. You are alive NOW *BREATHE*!

Much peace and blessings to you all. We love you!

BREATHE
An Anthology Compiled by Melinda Walker

Nichole Peters

Nichole Peters is an international motivational speaker known as the Believe Breakthrough Catalyst, a CEO, and the founder of Women of Love, Power, and Respect, Women Warriors Who Makes It ROCK, Believe Warriors Magazine and Believe In Your Dreams Publishing. Nichole is the senior executive producer of The Motivational Lounge radio show, and the national bestselling author of *A Woman of Love, Power, & Respect*, and the #1 best-selling author of *Women Warriors Who Make It Rock*.

Nichole believes in nurturing beautiful souls. Determined to teach downtrodden women and youth the power of self-love, she facilitates workshops and social media coaching for organizations, galas, conferences, retreats, and churches which encourages people to claim their blessings and live up to their greatness within. Her branding gifts and talent have reached the attention of many around the world. Nichole has coached hundreds of women and men to become best-selling authors. Nichole has been seen in the Huffington Post, VoiceAmerica, Amazon blogs, and Empowered Network Connections. In the last decade, Nichole has witnessed *manifestation* like never before. She believed and now has a social media following of almost 60,000 followers.

The youngest of nine children, Nichole was born and raised in a very small town called Bogalusa, Louisiana (sixty-three miles north of New Orleans). Nichole has experienced many wrong turns and hardships in life, but she has never lost hope nor stopped believing she would one day serve a greater purpose. As a result, God has not only blessed her with four amazing, beautiful children, but He brought her the love of her life and revealed to her to go after her childhood dreams to become a writer.

Nichole is also a wellness and beauty advocate. She is the owner of Ebullience 7 Spa. She is a die-hard advocate for domestic violence survivors. Nichole reaches out to different safe houses for abused women and delivers a message to let every woman know, "She is beautiful, strong, and can live off true love, not abuse."

"I have always loved God, but as a youth, I never truly embraced His teachings. In 2010, I decided to put HIM first in my life. I promised God, that no matter what storms I came across, no matter what the enemy tried to do, this would be our New Beginning and I would NEVER stop giving Him praise—no matter what. I will NEVER GIVE UP AGAIN!"

Contact Nichole at:

www.facebook.com/luvpowerrespect
www.twitter.com/luvpowerrespect
believeinnyourdreamsproductions@gmail.com

I Took a Deep Breath and I Let It Go
By: Melinda Walker

Growing up as the youngest of two daughters was very challenging. The enemy started working in my life at a young age. Being the youngest, I got a chance to see my sister at an older age. She was the predecessor who went before me. She and I were like night and day. She is extroverted and I am introverted. She gets a push from the outside and I get pleasure with being alone. I saw and experienced a lot growing up. My sister was light-skinned with pretty brown eyes that changed with her mood. She was always pretty. Everybody knew TJ. I, on the other hand, was always known as the dark one, the not-so-pretty one, who kept to herself. No one really knew me until I grew up. My sister was immediately accepted by family and friends, but I felt the sting of rejection often.

My mother loved us the same. I was the homebody who never gave my mom any problems, but my sister was totally the opposite. I clung to my mom and my sister clung to my grandmother. My grandmother was always there for my sister when she was put out, and that was often. She eventually moved in and stayed with my grandmother. My mom started working several jobs, which pushed me to have to spend several days and nights at my grandmothers. We did not bond right away, but as time progressed, she put aside the personal feelings she had toward me because of skin color. She saw that I was humble and pliable. I would obey and do what she told me to do. You just had to know Gladys Bee Coachman. Those on Church Street know exactly what I mean.

My grandmother started bringing me to Sunday school and church. I made St. Paul AME my church home. I went there all of my childhood. I still felt like I was the oddball in the family and it affected my self-esteem as a child. I felt like the black sheep of the family, all because I wasn't pretty enough. My mom and I were the only dark ones in our immediate family and we felt the difference. It destroyed my self-esteem. I had an older cousin who called me Grace Jones, and oh, did that make me feel some kind of way. My self-esteem took hit after hit, and I did not have anyone to protect me from the attitude and actions of others.

The only man who gave me value was my father. I could remember my father coming to see me at my grandmother's house and I would sit on his lap. He would tell me I was his girl and how much he loved me. One day, when I was around seven years old—I remember it like it was yesterday—my grandmother walked to our house on Liberty Drive and told me, my sister, and my mom that he had been murdered. I was devastated, and it left me with this huge void in my heart. I had no one to tell me I was pretty or I was loved. I went through life wondering: If he was still alive, would things have been different for me? I was a daddy's girl and I loved my father. When I lost him, it affected my life in a great way. I had no man to validate me. I had to grow up seeing only one side of love, and I could not recognize the real love of a man. I had no one to protect me against the hurt and disappointments of relationships.

My mother suffered as a woman greatly through failed relationships with men. She also suffered from low self-esteem and abuse issues. That caused an imbalance in her life. Her character was shaped by hurt and unresolved issues. Her capacity to bond and to love deeply were affected, so we never had that mother/daughter relationship, where I could go to her about any issues I was dealing with.

BREATHE
An Anthology Compiled by Melinda Walker

I remember playing house with my cousins and neighborhood friends. We experimented with touching and kissing. I was in a place where my sexuality was being challenged. I experimented with kissing a girl and I could have gone both ways. My mother worked sometimes three jobs at a time, so I was left to myself often. My sister was four years older, and she had her friends and was an extrovert, so her activities were always out and about.

I remember being sexually abused. I've never told anyone until this day. I held the hurt of life on the inside. That experience affected me. I got rejected often by guys. I felt I wasn't pretty enough, but I knew I had a pretty shape and my personality was inviting, and I was attractive. I used what I had to get what I wanted, and it worked. I became promiscuous and just wanted to be loved by the opposite sex. I was taken advantage of as a young girl. I had no one to pour into my life and give me direction. I didn't have anyone to tell me my body was a prized possession. The older men took advantage of me and I didn't know how to say no.

I went through many stages growing up. I found an outlet to my life and that was dancing. I got a crew together, which was my family, and we started dancing on the Extravaganza every year. I calmed down from the here-and-there relationships. I started dating this guy who was older, but a good guy. It was good until he got another girl pregnant and that was a deal breaker. I let that go. I started dating another guy around my age this time, and we dated for a while. I thought he might be the one. I began noticing he would not make it known we were together as boyfriend and girlfriend. I did go to his house, I met his family, but to the outside world, he was ashamed of me. He was a popular guy, nice physique, a football player. I remember when it was time for him to go to his football banquet. He told me one of his cousins told him not to take me, that I wasn't good enough to go with him and I would make him look bad. That crushed my spirit and my self-esteem took another hit. I was only fourteen years old and he was sixteen years old.

Then I found out I was pregnant. This was a shocker. I hadn't given my mom any trouble, but this broke her heart. I didn't have a say in the matter. She knew she could not help me. I was very smart and doing well in school, so she made the decision for me to get an abortion. This was a traumatic turn in my life. The depression really sank in. I thought God wouldn't forgive me. I felt I was hell bound. It was hard to forgive myself growing up with that guilt.

My grandmother saw I was withdrawing from church. She began to see a change in me. She started taking more time with me. She took me to the stores and bought me new dresses and shoes. She started making sure I was at Sunday school and choir rehearsals. She made it a point that I went to Vacation Bible School every summer. She took me to the prayer breakfast for women and different functions in the church. She made sure I worked in the church, serving communion (even though I ate more than I served). She took me to the annual conventions. She even made sure my sister and I ate three meals a day while my mother worked multiple jobs. She saved my life, and I thank her for that.

I was able to make it through high school without any more hiccups. The relationship I had with the guy I got pregnant by didn't last. He allowed a smooth-talking, tall, and handsome man who liked every part of me to take my heart. He wasn't ashamed of me. He took me places and was proud to have me. Eventually, I made a decision to exit one relationship and enter another one. I just liked the way I felt. I felt wanted, I felt pretty, and I was given value. I met my husband. We started dating from the summer of my senior year and we were married with a daughter a year after my graduation in 1991. We both were young and inexperienced. He was raised by his mother as well. He didn't have a father in his life and neither did I. We grew up together through trial and error.

I did pay a great price for a tall and handsome man. We went through so many challenges as a young couple. He didn't know what he was signing up for. He didn't understand what having a family meant. I didn't understand what having a husband meant. I'd never seen a good marriage work out in my life. I saw a lot of hurt and pain. I experienced a lot of hurt and pain that was kept on the inside for years. My breath was taken before I even got started in life. So, we experimented on one another.

My attitude was horrible. The inside started coming out in my character. I lived in this protective shell. I wasn't going to be talked to like a nobody without a reaction. I decided within myself he had one more time to mess up and I was out. I had all these preconceived notions going into the marriage. He introduced me to his God. I was introduced to church by my grandmother and church kept me busy and out of trouble, but he introduced me to Jesus. I started attending services every time the doors opened. I started learning my role as a wife and he started learning his role as a husband. We both start learning about love, forgiveness, and repentance. We started experiencing measures of deliverance, and we were ready to move forward.

I started growing a little faster than him. I was able to lay down my past. I was able to let go of the world. God began to chisel away the depression, the wall of indifference. He started filling my heart with love and forgiveness. I was letting my guards down. Then the enemy started hitting me where it hurt: my marriage. My husband was born into this generation cursed with lust. The same spirit got his daddy killed at the age of twenty-eight. My husband battled it throughout our marriage. I had two children by this time, and quitting for me was not an option. I refused to allow my children to suffer through what I'd suffered as a child. I made up my mind I would give my children what I didn't have: two parents who loved them.

My husband has always been challenged in that area of his life because he's very nice and hardworking and looks good, and that made him an easy target for women who are designed to shake up someone's marriage. By any means necessary, they will try to destroy a home. We were ten years into the marriage and I was pregnant with our last baby. He sat me down and told me he had gotten another woman pregnant. I didn't have words to express how I felt. I had two children, ages nine and seven, and one almost there. I was too numb to cry. I went back to that little girl who was rejected growing up.

My self-esteem was at zero. My attitude really got bad. I was between a rock and a very hard place. I grew very cold and evasive. I was very bitter on the inside. Forgiveness was far and few between. Many times, I questioned my husband's love for me. I questioned the God in him. I questioned the love of God. I was full of questions. I felt that I'd caused the infidelity. I went back to the little girl with low self-esteem who felt like she was just not good enough. I went into a deep depression. My attitude grew worse. I was angry with everyone. I was told to forgive.

I struggled with the decision of remaining in the marriage. I was told to forgive for me, not for my husband. I gave him pure hell.

I gave him no respect. I lost all trust. It had gotten so bad that I was at the verge of nervous breakdown. I started crying uncontrollably and couldn't stop. This was a daily thing. I started eating uncontrollably and put on about twenty-five extra pounds. I just didn't care any more. My marriage took a hit, and the enemy rushed in like a flood to kill my purpose, to kill my desires, and to destroy my marriage. I had to make a decision. Everyone was saying, "Lynn, you've come too far. Don't let the enemy destroy everything you have built."

By that time, I was ten years into my marriage with three children. What was I going to do? I knew I couldn't remain in this state. I humbled myself so I could pray and ask God for direction. I simply asked God for myself, "What do I do?" I told God I had the right to leave and it would not be held to my account. I asked God to release me from this hurt and this pain. He simply said, "This was necessary." I looked up the word necessary and it means it was needed, it was essential, it had to happen. That was mind-blowing to me, but I knew I could not argue with God.

As I humbled myself, I allowed the spirit of God to wash my heart. The process of forgiveness began. I accepted the grace of God in my life. He began to put salve to my soreness. He began to bring restoration to my brokenness. As He was dealing with me, He also was dealing with my husband. He began to mend the brokenness of our marriage. We accepted the counseling we needed. I accepted the answers God gave me. He told me to stay and He would restore my marriage. I took a deep breath and I let it go.

BREATHE
An Anthology Compiled by Melinda Walker

Melinda Anese Walker

Melinda Anese Walker, BKA Lynn, was born and raised in Bogalusa, LA. She is the youngest of two girls. She graduated from high school in 1991 and completed two years of college. She later moved to Mississippi and was united in matrimony with her husband of twenty-five years. They reside in Hattiesburg and have been there for over twenty years. They have three children together.

Melinda serves as an Evangelist at the Outreach Fellowship Revival Center. She has been serving for twenty-five years under the leadership of Pastor Jessie Holloway and the late Barbara Jean Holloway. She has been a speaker on WJDR 98.3 for over a decade. They spread the Word of God throughout several counties. She is currently a healthcare provider with Broadpath Healthcare Solutions. She is pursuing a career as a Health and Wellness Coach. She is a certified Life/Purpose Coach and a Happiness Coach. She owns Comfortable in One's Own Skin, an online boutique.

She is a co-author in the anthology Women Warriors Who Make It Rock. She is the author and spiritual compiler of her own Anthology, Breathe. She is a firm believer that with hard work, confidence, conviction, and belief in one's self, you can achieve anything, even if the odds are stacked against you.

Contact Melinda at:

Abundantlife2018@gmail.com
Melindawalker73@yahoo.com
Comfortableinonesownskin.com
https://comingfullcircle.itworks.com
 @melinda.walker.9085.facebook.com
Melindawalker73.instagram.com/p/pUXFBuE7PO/
Melindawalker73.twitter.com

Prescription for Survival:
Blood of Faith in My Spiritual Veins
By: Sarah E. Anderson

Growing up, I had the best life any child could imagine. I was born and raised in the church, got good grades in school, and had everything I could possibly need: hot food on the table and a roof always over my head. As a young person, I had big dreams and plans for my life. As a child, I wanted to become a teacher, caretaker, and a massage therapist. Therefore, I always said, "When I grow up, I will go straight to college and accomplish my dreams."

However, God had other plans for my life. Not knowing what my future was really going to look like, I went on living life as though my blueprint would override God's path to my future. Isn't that what most young people my age do? So, you can say, I was not abnormal in my thinking. What the Lord ultimately showed me was I was not NORMAL. Now that makes me laugh out loud as I am looking back on what I had to endure.

Well, there I was at the age of eighteen, about three months pregnant and a senior in high school. As a high school senior, I was doing exactly what any other student about to graduate would be doing. You guessed it: I was completing college applications, trying to find money for college, preparing to participate in graduation activities, prom, and all the normal things high school seniors do. Yes, I was super excited! I was as close to my dreams as I could be. All the things I'd imagined as a little girl were on track to becoming reality. In all my excitement, many doubted me and many even laughed because I had become a statistic—another pregnant teen.

BREATHE
An Anthology Compiled by Melinda Walker

Although I knew what others were thinking, it increased my desire to achieve my personal goals. I made sure I was at school on time every single day. I was dressed to impress. I was pretty popular among my peers. I was well on my way to success. My mind was so far from what I was about to experience.

One day, I began having very excruciating toothaches while at school. The pain would only happen while I was in school. I expressed to my mom the pain I was feeling, and she insisted we go to the doctor the following day. We walked into the dentist, signed in, and waited to be seen by the doctor. We sat for about thirty minutes before we were finally called to the back to take x-rays. After taking the x-rays, the nurse escorted us to the room where I would be examined once the x-rays came back. After sitting in the examination chair for about fifteen minutes, the doctor finally came in with the results. I had an infection. I was given pain medicine and infection medicine and was told to come back in about seven to fourteen days.

I took the prescriptions to get them filled and began to take the medicine to help with the pain. Nothing seemed to be working! I did what I was told, took the medication as prescribed, and came back to the dentist for my follow-up appointment so I could see where things were concerning my infection. After fourteen days of taking medication and following the prescribed instructions, the pain was intensifying. Things were getting worse with each day. After attending my follow-up appointment, the dentist gave me the same diagnosis: an abscess with an infection. I was livid and wanted a second opinion.

Leaving the dentist upset, I knew something was wrong, but no one seemed to understand. I expressed my feelings to my mom and told her I wanted a second opinion. Knowing I had to be at school the next day, I went home, ate dinner, and got ready for bed.

Weeks passed by and my mom finally found another dentist who would give as an opportunity for a second opinion. An appointment was scheduled and we were ready to go in. Walking into the new dentist, I felt like there was hope. I signed in, sat down, and waited for my name to be called. About fifteen minutes after signing in, I was called to the back for an x-ray. After the x-ray, I was escorted to the waiting room to wait until the results came back. About ten minutes later the results were in, and I was called to the back again to discuss what was seen on the x-ray.

Understanding everything the doctor told me at that point was very clear. I felt what he was saying to me was comforting, as if he felt the pain I felt. The doctor then prescribed for me to do the same thing as the first one, but for some reason, I felt I could trust this doctor. The doctor told me to go home, take the pain meds and antibiotics, and return in seven days for a second x-ray.

Seven days passed, and I was back at the dentist to do a follow-up appointment. Although I didn't feel any changes, I knew something still felt seriously wrong. I signed in, sat down, and waited to be called. After sitting for only a few minutes, I was called to the back to do a second x-ray, then was sent back to the waiting area until the results came back. I did not know what was going on. It took a long time for a nurse or even the doctor to come tell me what was going on. Minutes later, the doctor called my mom and me to the back to discuss the findings of the x-ray.

The doctor held up the previous week's x-ray to the current week's x-ray and said, "Compared to last week's x-ray, your entire bone from your chin to your ear has deteriorated."

Immediately I was referred to the University of Illinois at Chicago College of Dentistry. Dr. D explained that what was happening was not normal dentistry and felt I needed a specialist because of the progression of the bone deterioration in the past seven days. Dr. D. made sure I would get the attention I needed, using every resource possible to connect me with a specialist. As promised, he connected me to Dr. K. at UIC College of Dentistry Maxillofacial Surgery Suite.

Rushing to UIC to meet with the specialist, it still had not dawned on me that things could be serious. As soon as I arrived at the facility and checked in, the team of doctors was awaiting to take me to one of the waiting rooms to start the process. After going through a round of questions and a physical examination of my mouth, the doctor noted that a biopsy was required. A sample of the tissue in my mouth was cut and prepared for processing. I might add, it left a pretty big hole in my gums to the point that I could see the roots of my teeth. Can you imagine brushing your teeth and seeing the roots of your teeth because the bone was completely gone? Neither could I.

A few days had passed since the biopsy. I kept my normal routine: getting ready for school, going to breakfast, then to music class, art, gym, science, lunch, and finite math. It was not until the finite math class that I received a phone call from the College of Dentistry Maxillofacial office. I asked permission from my teacher to answer the phone because we were not supposed to have a cellphone in class, but this was important. I answered the phone.

On the other end, someone said, "Hello, this is the nurse from UIC Hospital. May I speak with Sarah Anderson?"

I replied, "This is she."

BREATHE
An Anthology Compiled by Melinda Walker

She said, "We have the results of your biopsy and we need you to come in right away to discuss them."

I asked her if she could tell me over the phone because I was in school. She responded with an emphatic no and told me to get to the hospital as soon as possible. After receiving the nod to leave school, I hopped in my mom's car and drove to the hospital.

Walking into the hospital, I had no worries at all. I signed in and waited to be called. About ten minutes into signing in, I was called to the back. The doctor asked if I had come by myself. I let her know that, because I was eighteen years old, I did not need anyone with me. I asked the doctor to give it to me straight. However, the doctor refused to give me any information about my biopsy because she felt I needed to have some support.

I called my mom and got no answer. After so many attempts to call my mom with no answer, the doctor called and was able to connect with my mother and told her to drop whatever she was doing and get to the hospital as soon as possible. My mom did not have a vehicle because she had allowed me to drive her car to school that morning. However, my mother arrived so fast, you would have thought she'd flown in by jet.

When my mom arrived, we were placed in a small conference room to get the results of the biopsy. We sat down in the quiet room as the doctor pulled my chart up on the computer. The doctor turned to me and said, "I'm not going to sugarcoat anything, Sarah. You have stage 4 invasive squamous cell carcinoma in your lower right mandible." As the doctor was speaking, she said without hesitation, "We are going to take really good care of you. The first thing we must do is take care of the baby. The focus is on you having a healthy baby, then we will get to you."

All I could do was say okay because I really did not understand what cancer was, let alone stage 4. It wasn't until I heard my mom break down and say her dad had just died from the same cancer a few years ago that I began to cry. It just seemed so surreal at that point. I broke down! The devil was in my head telling me now it was my turn to die, just like my granddad. I was scared. I was hurt. I didn't know if my baby or I was going to make it. I was filled with all types of emotions. Leaving the hospital with that news was the worst feeling I could have felt. I was suddenly numb. I didn't want to talk, see, or even hear anything. I wanted to shut myself off from the world and just think about what had just happened to me.

As I took myself through these reflexive and reflective processes, I had so many questions. Out of all the questions, I never once ask God, "WHY ME?" I reflected on the goals and dreams I had for myself, but then I realized in that moment that it was NOT about MY PLANS; it was about GOD'S PURPOSE for my LIFE! All I could say was, WOW! God was about to show Himself strong. All I had ever been taught in the Scriptures and through watching living examples as a little girl in church was FAITH. I encourage every reader to take FAITH and walk through any aspect of negativity that is against his/her DIVINE PURPOSE. My testimony and final answer as to how I SURVIVED is the BLOOD of FAITH running through my SPIRITUAL VEINS!

BREATHE
An Anthology Compiled by Melinda Walker

Sarah Elisabeth Anderson: "Cancer Survivor through Faith"

Sarah Elisabeth Anderson, the youngest of three children, was born in Indianola, Mississippi, to Leroy and Carol Washington Anderson. Sarah, whose name means "Princess Consecrated to God", was brought up in the church and was taught to always trust God in everything. In 2000, Sarah and her mother relocated to Chicago. Since coming to Chicago, Sarah has stolen the hearts of most of her teachers, principals, and even her Pastor, Superintendent Michael Eaddy. Her genuine spirit and love for God often draws others to her without a sweat.

Chosen by Reverend Jesse L. Jackson and Rainbow PUSH, Sarah traveled to Ghana, West Africa, in 2008, an experience that would change her life forever. It was there where the Lord began to deal with her about her own life in the United States and how He wanted to use her. Although she did not understand exactly how the Lord would use her, she accepted the challenge.

In 2009, a graduating senior and four months pregnant, Sarah began to experience pain in her body. Her mother took her to the doctor time after time after time. In June 2009, the pain was so excruciating, Sarah convinced her mother to change doctors. It was in December 2009, Sarah would receive a diagnosis that rocked her entire world—STAGE 4 head and neck cancer. In October 2010, after going through extensive treatment and reconstruction, Sarah would receive a prognosis of CANCER FREE.

Although the odds were seemingly stacked against her, Thornton Township High School administration, counseling team, and teachers ensured Sarah would be able to receive her high school diploma, despite not being able to complete her senior year. She was unable to fully walk or be subjected to the heat of the sun. However, in May 2010, Thornton Township came to pick her up and drove her across the football stadium so she could receive her high school diploma. Today, Sarah is a junior, majoring in secondary math education at Grand Canyon University online. She is working on completing her book, titled *Cancer Survivor Through Faith*. In this writing, she will detail all the miraculous aspects of her battle with cancer as a teenager and a young mother. She has been gifted to write songs the Lord gives and will be soon completing her single, titled *I Made It Through*. The message behind the music is simply awesome.

She has a passion to help as many people as she possibly can while upholding a standard of holiness and righteous living. Sarah is committed to sharing with the world how the Lord used this disease to change her life for the better. She is committed to ministering to those who need to hear a message of hope, healing, inspiration, and FAITH in GOD. Sarah realizes her healing came only through her relationship with God and her willingness to KEEP THE FAITH.

Sarah is the mother of her miracle child, Navayah L'Faith Mayfield, without who the progression of the cancer may not have been realized as quickly. She credits her FAITH in GOD for her TOTAL HEALING.

Contact Sarah at:

Facebook:
https://m.facebook.com/2010topmodel?ref=Bookmarks

Sarah CancerSurvivor Anderson
https://m.facebook.com/keepthefaithtosurvive/?ref=bookmarks

Keep the Faith to Survive
Email/phone number: Keepthefaithtosurvive@yahoo.com
773-426-1570

Excess Baggage
By: Rita Taylor

Sometimes in life, circumstances happen. In light of the daily trials we call "life", life will sometimes cause us to question our purpose. About thirty years ago, my life circumstances caused me to let extra things attach to my self-esteem. I call those things excess baggage. Excess baggage can be anything we carry in our lives as a choice, things that cloud our view as to what we are called to do.

When I was twenty-one and supposedly in "love", I married a gentleman. I felt like my life was complete. After three years, I found myself devastated and headed to divorce court. I felt the sting of failure and despair. After some time of dealing with the fact that I was now a single mom, my self-esteem was compromised. I found myself dealing with one disappointment after another. Jealousy and depression are a few of the spirits I allowed in my life.

This is what I call excess baggage. It took a constant prayer life for me to realize that change was needed. I began to develop a prayer life and it was then that I could honestly be true to myself. I began to apply every biblical principle to my life and to my life's circumstances. I found me! Or did I?

God sent me a wonderful husband, whom I have been with for twenty-six years. After several years in this marriage, what I call lost baggage began to appear. Yes, the jealousy, depression, and low self-esteem crept back into the forefront of my life. I found myself re-examining what I was allowing to reenter my life. Constant self-examination and purification by the Holy Spirit kept me. It is a daily commitment not to pick up excess baggage. Don't get me confused: to have happiness, I'm not saying we need a man, or any other fleshly desire. What I am saying is, when we rid ourselves of excess baggage and find self-happiness, God will give you the desires of your heart.

Excess baggage can be anything we choose to take possession of. For me, it was low self-esteem. I felt I was a failure. These types of spirits do not align with the Word of God and His promises. As I meditated on the Word of God, I was reminded of a couple of examples. In Genesis, the third chapter and the first verse, Eve was faced with a choice. We are faced with choices on a daily basis. Will we choose good, or will we choose evil? Will we choose our fleshly desires, or will we choose to obey the command of God as it relates to our lives?

Remember, every negative choice comes with consequences. Eve decided to carry the baggage of disobedience. God afforded Eve the opportunity to enjoy the beauty of the garden. The instruction God gave was they could not eat from the tree of good and evil. We all know the command was given to Adam, not Eve. I am convinced that because they were connected, they both suffered the consequences of their disobedience.

Excess baggage will not only affect you, but everyone who is connected to you. The actions of Adam and Eve caused them to endure punishment. First, they were put out the garden. Second, they had to work for their food. These things came as a result of their excess baggage of disobedience.

Another passage that is dear to my heart is the story of David. David was a man after God's own heart, but David sinned greatly. David looked upon a beautiful woman named Bathsheba and desired her. The interesting thing about this is, this woman was not available. Covet and lust set up in David's heart. He wanted her and was willing to do whatever it took to get her—including murdering Bathsheba's husband. All because of David's excess baggage of coveting, lust, murder, and misused power, he had years of suffering. Everything in David's life was affected by this event.

We cannot allow life's trials to tempt us into carrying unnecessary baggage. I encourage you to only carry the necessary items needed for your journey, for your destiny. Extra baggage can cost you everything. When traveling, most airlines will allow one carry-on. Usually your carry-on has the essentials you may need for the journey. There is a charge for extra and overweight baggage. I sometimes overpack. When I overpack and arrive at the check-in, the attendant weighs my baggage. If my baggage weighs too much, then I am charged an extra fee! Are you paying for carrying excessive baggage?

When I dealt with low self-esteem, I was carrying baggage I didn't need. In our lives, we tend to overpack our lives with things that are not designed for our journey. Excess baggage will cost us. It will weigh us down spiritually. Adam, Eve, David, myself, and so many others have carried excess baggage. Excess baggage causes us to experience detours in a pre-set journey.

My life has been filled with mountains of emotions that affected my decisions. I am grateful for God's grace that restored me to my rightful place. Because of my excess baggage, I suffered years of uncertainty. Let me ask you a question: What excess baggage are you carrying? Will it assist you in getting to your destiny? And finally, was it designed for your life? Are you carrying depression? Are you carrying hatred? Are you carrying anger? Are you carrying lust? Are you carrying low self-esteem? Are you carrying jealousy? Are you disappointed in yourself and feeling hopeless?

BREATHE
An Anthology Compiled by Melinda Walker

Jeremiah 29:11 says, "I know the plans I have for you, declares the Lord, to prosper you and give you hope for the future." Are you carrying low self-esteem, as I was? This baggage comes from the remnants of your past. No matter how insignificant you may feel, be encouraged to know that God specializes in brokenness. The challenge for us all is to let go of our past problems, our past cares, our past concerns, our past mistakes, and our past failures. This baggage does nothing but weigh us down.

Hebrews 12:1 says, "Let us strip off every weight that slows us down, especially the sin that so easily trips us up. And let us run with endurance the race God has set before us." The weight of excess baggage stops us from getting to our destined place in God. It also causes us to sin and suffer the consequences of our actions. Everything we are connected to effects everybody we are connected to. We must check in all unneeded and unwanted baggage at the feet of Jesus. Maybe you are faced with a choice to let go of something that wasn't designed for your life.

I felt so dependent on my excess baggage that I hid behind the polished clothes and painted face. I didn't need the excess—I wanted it! It was a comfortable place for me. It wasn't until I became truthful with myself and released my fears to God that I felt free. Galatians 5:22-23 says, "But the fruit of the Spirit is love, joy, peace, forbearance, and self-control, against such things there is no law."

I want to pray with you, that you will be able to let go of all the baggage that is not ordained for your life. I pray God will give you strength to dispel the myths of the enemy that keep you bound and entangled in carrying a load that is not yours. I want to pray that the excess in your life be replaced with the godly essentials you need to sustain your journey. By letting the excess weight go, we are able to be free and confident in God to *BREATHE*! I love the song by Jonny

BREATHE
An Anthology Compiled by Melinda Walker

Diaz: "Come and rest at my feet and be, chaos calls but all you really need is to just breathe...JUST *BREATHE!*"

Rita L. Taylor

Rita is a native of Fort Worth, Texas, and is the second child of five children born to Bishop Willis and Lady Rita Pace. Rita has been married to her husband Pastor Christopher F. Taylor for twenty-six years. She has six beautiful children: Christeyun, Roy, Ashleigh, Christopher, Matthew, and Trystan. She also has three grandchildren: Ryleigh, Jaxson, and Kingsley. Besides wearing the hats of wife, mother, and grandmother, Rita is a key figure in the secular arena. She operates the Princess Boutique Charm School where she mentors young ladies ages thirteen and up, teaching etiquette and sustaining and fostering healthy esteem and morals.

Rita is the author of the *WOW (Working on Womanhood)* etiquette curriculum workbook for girls. She is also an Amazon bestselling co-author of the book *Women Warriors Who Make It Rock,* as well the author of the upcoming breast cancer awareness book, *Not Just in October*, due out October 2018. She is the co-founder, along with her husband, of the Agape Christian Learning Academy. Rita also hosted a radio talk show called, *Inside the Heart with Lady T*. The show was an open forum, discussing pertinent Christian issues. Rita served as the personal assistant to David and Tamela Mann, also known as the Browns. She is co-partners with Brand1 entertainment, where she handles personal accounts for other celebrities. Rita is the co-owner of The Taylor Group Inc., a full-service company that specializes in media, publicity, and personal assisting.

Rita is, along with her husband, the co-founder of New Direction Ministries, which is a healing ministry offering Christian servanthood training. She has served as a pastor, armor bearer, counselor, publicist, mentor, spiritual advisor, teacher, prophet, and friend. Her ministry serves as a conduit to heal hurting and weary women. Rita is a woman of profound intercession coupled with a passion to heal hurting people. However, she is first and foremost a worshiper! She is very confident of her calling and assignment in this 21st century. She intentionally stays reminded of Jeremiah 29:11: "For I know the plans I have for you, declares the Lord, plans to prosper you and not to harm you, plans to give you hope and a future."

Rita declares she is still "UNDER CONSTRUCTION"! She is convinced nothing happens under the sun that is not ordained by God. We have to travel different routes to accomplish our individual goals of success. Life is uncertain, but one thing is for sure: We are all being shaped and molded to be our intended design, the design that was decided before the beginning of time.

I pray that you'll enjoy traveling with me on my journey as I allow God to rid my life of the excess baggage. I am compelled daily to travel lightly. Through our daily lives, things will try to attach themselves to us, but if it's not ordained by God, it should remain UNCLAIMED BAGGAGE.

Contact Rita at:
Facebook: Rita Pace Taylor
Email: iamrita@thetaylorgroupinc.org

Once the Healing Began, I Was Able to Breathe
By: Arlene Walker

At the age of six, I can remember running behind my mother as she was running for her life because my father was trying to kill her. That very same night, my father was killed by my uncle. John 10:10 says, "The devil comes to steal, kill, and destroy." We were left without a father, and my mother had to raise seven children on her own. My mother was violently abused for as long as I could remember. One thing that helped my mother to overcome all she endured was her faith and trust in GOD. My mother was a great woman of God. She walked in righteousness before her children and was a great example for us to follow when it came to serving God. She was also a great provider because she always depended on God for our needs. Philippians 4:19 says, "My God shall supply all my needs according to His riches and glory in Christ Jesus."

At the age of forty-nine, my mother died of cancer. I did not want to live any longer after her death. The only thing that kept me from committing suicide was I had a five-year-old son I had to take care of, and I didn't feel that anyone would care for him like I would. At that point in my life, I had to grab a hold of God and not let go. I would go to church on Sundays and cry through the whole service. My mother was my best friend. We had a bond that was unbreakable. She was my rock, and I felt like I had nothing else to live for after her death.

I went through many hard trials just as my mother did, but because of the faith and trust in God that I'd witnessed from her, I made it through. There were times when I was without food and water in my home, but I would find something in my house to give someone who was in need and it always came back to me triple. I learned that giving was a way to survive. Luke 6:38 says, "Give and it shall be given unto you, pressed down, and shaken together running over, shall men give into your bosom." There were times when I would sit down and just make a list of the debts I had. After making the list, every morning I would quote scriptures from the Bible and remind God of His Word and promises to me. My favorite was Matthew 7:7: "Ask and it shall be given unto you, seek and you shall find, and knock and the door will be opened unto you." Before I knew it, that debt was gone.

My faith in God has carried me through some very difficult times. While going through a failed marriage, I went through some of the hardest things I feel a person can bear. My husband and I were not equally yoked. What I mean by that is we did not have the same mindset. We both had different lifestyles and we could not get along. Amos 3:3 says, "How can two walk together unless they agree?" I really didn't understand the meaning of that until marriage. I didn't agree with ninety percent of what he said and I am a believer; neither did he agree with me. The Bible also says in Ephesians 5:25, "Husbands, love your wives like Christ loves the Church." I am not saying my husband did not love me; he loved me the only way he knew how. If your husband does not have the love of God in his heart, do not expect him to love you like Christ loves the Church because he does not have it in him to do so. Ephesians 5:22-23 also says, "Wives submit yourself to your own husband." It is very hard to submit to a man who is not submitted to God or anyone else.

These are just some examples of what I went through in the marriage that were very difficult for me, and him as well. After the terrible loss of the marriage, I found a secret place in God that brought me through those hard times. Psalms 91:1 says, "He that dwelleth in the secret place of the Most High shall abide under the shadow of the Almighty." This secret place was and still is my bathtub. When I am in distress and troubled, this is the place where I go and cry out to God. This is a place of refuge for me. This is a place where I always go to *BREATHE*. This is a place where I can go and release all built-up anger, hurt, and disappointment. I just relax and find comfort in Jesus. It soothes me and gives me the strength to persevere through some of the hardest battles I feel a person can bear. Life has a way of pushing you to a place sometimes where you feel you cannot and do not want to go on.

Because of disobedience to God and His Word, I have had to go through much unnecessary heartache and pain. If you are not willing to obey, life will teach you, and if life teaches you, it is a hard lesson. God is not a forceful God. He loves us so much that He gives us free will, but there are consequences for our actions. Isaiah 1:19-20 says, "If you be willing and obedient, you shall eat the good of the land. But if you refuse and rebel, ye shall be devoured with the sword. For the mouth of the LORD hath spoken it." I was once searching for people and things, trying to fill a void I had within me. That void was only filled by God. I am at a place in my life now that I just want to do God's will, and most of all, I am seeking Him daily to know His will for my life.

I know there are young women out there who are trying to find their way in this life. I would like for you to know that life is full of choices and these choices will determine your future. A relationship with God will lead you in the right direction and help you to make the right choices. Pray daily for direction and guidance. Ask God to give you spiritual eyes that you can see, ears that you can hear, and an understanding heart. Pray daily for wisdom, knowledge, and understanding, and ask Him to help you to apply it to your life. He will do just that.

Once I began to get in God's Word and renew my mind, change started to happen for me. If you never change the way you think, you will never change the way you live. Renewing your mind will change the way you live and give you a better quality of life. If you never renew your mind, your life will remain the same. You will continue to do the same things over and over, and wonder why things and situations never change. If your mind changes, your life will change. You will no longer want to continue to do things that are of no value for you. Change will only come from getting in God's Word daily. Meditating and studying brings about a change. Romans 12:2 says, "Be not conformed to this world, but be ye transformed by the renewing of your mind, that you may prove what is that good, acceptable, and perfect will of God. There is no better place to be than the will of God." Romans 8:31 says, "If God be for us, who in the world can be against us?" With God on our side, we have already won.

I honor God not just with my lips, but with my life. When I am going through difficult situations and trying times, I know that the strength that is within me, Jesus Christ, will help me make it through. That strength gives me peace; it gives me endurance to go on when I feel like I can't. I'm so grateful to Christ for saving me and delivering me daily. I thank God for the plans He has for me, plans to prosper me and to give me a good future. I am so grateful. I hold on to that promise with my life because without Christ, I am nothing in this world.

We all must leave this world one day and we will not just cease to exist, but we will meet our King. I want to hear Him say, "Well done; come on in." To God be the glory for all the things He has done and continues to do for me daily. Choose ye this day whom you will serve. As for me, I will serve the Lord with gladness and a willing heart.

Arlene Walker

Arlene Walker was born in Crystal Springs, Mississippi, but was raised in Prentiss, Mississippi. She is presently fifty-one years of age. She is the mother of one child, Juan Dewayne Walker, whom she loves dearly. She has a very sweet and loving daughter-in-law and one grandson. She is the third child of seven children. She accepted Jesus Christ as her Lord and Savior at the age of nineteen.

She started her membership with Outreach Fellowship Revival Center, where she is to this day still a member. This church is where she has learned how to be faithful and trust in God. She learned about discipline, how to press her way through hard times and situations, how to be faithful and committed, and most of all, she was taught the Word of God, which delivers her daily.

Arlene has worked with the public for about seventeen years. She worked with the school system for eight years, teaching the youth, and she has also worked in banking. She is presently working with Medicare to assist the elderly and disabled.

Stop, Drop & Quantum Leap into Redemption and Your Destiny
By: Derricka Holliman

Life itself will teach you many lessons. We must embrace, enjoy, and learn from our journey. We always say, "If I knew what I know now, I would have made better decisions, or my life would be different." In other words, I shoulda, woulda, coulda. As the old folks say, keep living and the retest will come. As time passes initially, we should have learned and gotten wiser to make better decisions because when you know better, you do better. Clearly, at times, we know better, but choose to do wrong. Sometimes, we take for granted what wrong and bad actions lead to, or the consequences behind them.

I use to be the head of my life. I did what I wanted to do to satisfy myself. I went down many roads that were dead ends. I was young, ignorant, and curious. I saw many hard times, sad days, and gloomy nights. I was weak to temptations and fell for many things like drugs, tobacco, men, and wrong wants, thoughts, and desires. I was also full of hate, anger, and frustrations. My mind was troubled with the wrong way of thinking.

Immature thinking leads to foolish actions and influences, and caused me to feel the void of sadness and many other storms raging in my life. I smoked marijuana to comfort my pain. With the stress of everyday life, I turned to cigarettes, which became my right-hand friend. I couldn't live with them or without them, if you know what I mean. Self-relevance began to wear me down and left me feeling weak, and I began to drink Red Bull for energy. All three of these bad habits that I thought were stress relievers ended up adding stress to my life. I was under the influence that I not only wanted them but had to have them. I was looking for love and comfort in all the wrong places, ending up with more problems and worse situations.

I'm a mother of three children, and I had to change and change quick. I didn't want to lead them down the wrong road. As parents, we are their biggest mentors. They are watching us. I had a teenage son who I had to lead by example. I couldn't tell him not to smoke or that it wasn't good for him if he witnessed me doing it. Children don't do what we say; they do what they see. It was time to lose and say goodbye to the bad habits I had picked up along my journey for my own sake and for my family's.

I was tired of being tired of my reckless life. I tried many things to fix my problems. I tried everything but God. I knew of the Problem Solver, the Heart Mender, and the Mind Regulator. I prayed to Him sometimes, but I didn't have a daily devotion with Him. I heard of Him through other people, but I didn't know Him on an intimate level for myself. I had a part-time relationship with Him. I was known as a CEO. I went to church on Christmas, Easter, and one other Sunday out of the year. I was in charge and the head of my own life. I was disobedient, I had a lack of trust, no faith, and I was spiritually dead. I was living with no sense of direction, also known as a drifter. I was living however the wind blew, sadly thinking, if I was to leave this earth, I was going to heaven—but I was headed straight to hell.

It was time for me to STOP and quantum leap into redemption. I was looking for love in all the wrong places. I was down in a deep, dark valley. I knew if I continued to do the same things, I would only reap the same results. I couldn't do it without God. I had to stop and turn from my wicked ways, drop down on my knees, and surrender my life to Christ. I could no longer live without Him being the head of my life. I needed Him to lead and guide me. I had to put my confidence, trust, and belief in Him, knowing He is my refuge and strength ever-present help in time of trouble. I surrendered with a sincere heart, looking and seeking Christ with expectation for Him to change, rearrange, and transform me. I began to pray more, developing a prayer life. God began to strengthen my spirit. My mind began to change along with the desires of my heart, my wants and needs. I began to yearn for a good church home. God led me to a church named Harvest Worship Center.

Harvest Worship Center was just what I wanted and needed: a fairly-new, small church with an intimate spiritual atmosphere, with pastors after God's own heart. I could see my spiritual life growing and developing into a beautiful new life. I was in a place where my soul was being fed. God could use me and my mistakes. I was receiving wisdom and knowledge with an understanding. It was a place of good ground where I could plant and sow seeds for my life and watch God transform me. My relationship with God began to get serious. I no longer had a part-time relationship; it was now a full-time relationship with Him. My feelings were changing toward God. I began to fear Christ and wanted to please Him. I wanted to seek Him and spend more time with Him on a daily basis. Waking up and going to bed with Him on my mind is such a wonderful experience. I then knew I was falling in love with Jesus. I needed and wanted more of Him.

Fear was developed and conviction started up. As I attended Harvest Worship Center, my pastors received and delivered the Word just how God instructed them to, speaking life, teaching, and pushing us to the next level. Harvest went on a fast that would forever change my life. I declared I was proceeding with expectations to receive freedom from my bad habits. Liberty was mine to walk in. I knew I could escape through God and He would rescue me. On this twenty-one-day fast, I turned to Him during every ungodly desire. I remembered my bad habits: weed, cigarettes, and Red Bulls. When I thought of them, I turned to Him; when I desired them, I turned to Him. I prayed for God to take the desire, taste, wants, and thoughts away, and He did! Chains were broken, burdens lifted, and my mind was regulated. I don't even think about those things any more. My desire is to be more like Him, to get to know Him in many ways for myself. I know He is a deliverer, a way maker, a healer, and so much more. I must stay yoked to Him.

As I look over my life, I've been through many trials and tribulations that I've overcome through the grace of God. I was underserving, but His love covered and kept me through car accidents, different additions, adultery, anger, anxiety, the death of a child, depression, divorce, doubt, and drug abuse. He said He will never leave us or forsake us in the valley. *BREATHE* on me, Lord. Going through the storm, *BREATHE* on me. Coming out on top of the mountains, *BREATHE* on me. So, remember, if God be for us, who can be against us? Nobody but ourselves. Encourage yourself and *BREATHE*. Redemption is yours to walk in and God's destiny for you. God has a purpose and plan for our lives, and He is more than willing to show exactly how He wants to use us for His glory.

Derricka Holliman

Derricka Holliman was born in Joliet, Illinois. She moved to Hattiesburg, Mississippi, when she was nine years old. She is the only daughter of three children. She is a devoted wife with two beautiful daughters and one son. She is a beauty specialist and has been a stylist for seventeen years and owns her own salon. She specializes in hair weaves, up do's, dry wraps, and flat irons, among many other styles. If you're considering going natural, she can help you with making the transition. She specializes in silk wraps and natural styles.

She is a member of Harvest Worship Center under the leadership of Pastor Kareem and Lashun Singleton. She serves as lead usher, an intercessor, and serves on the pastor's aid committee. Her ministry is for those who are dealing with addictions and strongholds. God has called her to minister the Word and inspire other women with the things He has delivered her from. She uses her salon as a tool for ministering and listening to the hearts of women on a daily basis. God has called her out as a leader. Weeping may endure for a night, but JOY comes in the morning. As a co-author in this anthology, God has caused morning to come into her life. Good morning.

Contact Derricka at:

derricka.scott@yahoo.com
(601) 310-0923

When the Enemy Rushed in Like a Flood I Decided to Exhale
By: Schynies Williamson

I lived a life that had me far out in the world because I had no understanding of God's vision, which made it difficult to fight satan. My mind was undeveloped and needed to be renewed in God due to my focus being lost on who I was in Him. It allowed my flesh to conflict with the spiritual realm and had me functioning improperly. Although it wasn't determined where I was going in life, satan wanted me to be blinded in my situation and looking backward (1 Thessalonians 5:9-22). Satan will keep the vision of God closed to you if you do not learn to let go of hurts, bitterness, and un-forgiveness, and to properly function in God (2 Corinthians 11:3). The Israelites couldn't come from negative thinking because they had a negative attitude that cost them to lose focus of where they were going. They lost ground with God because of their flesh (Proverbs 23:7).

Satan wanted me to feel as if there was no way out of my dilemma, and he didn't want me to live in God's love, share my story with others, and help them to gain access to the knowledge of God (Peter 4:12). The Ephesus Baptist Church stated that Paul rested in his contentment in God because he knew he had full control and he didn't feel that he was a victim, nor did he pity his situation (Philippians 4:10-13). Remember, you can become a product of what you are living, or you can break the cycle of the perception of what satan says you are and walk in who God said you are in Him instead.

Matthew 22:14 tells us that many are called, but few are chosen. Why? Because when God is calling us, we can't hear Him because of undeveloped ears and undeveloped minds. Satan will take control of your destiny and change your course, make the grace of God die in you, and make you become spiritually dead in him because he hates you just like he hates God. If you have not developed a solid ground in Christ, you will live a dysfunctional life and become spiritually paralyzed with no foundation to stand in God.

I was one of five children born to the late Dolphin Williamson. He enlisted in the Army, serving his country, but was living a lie behind closed doors. He was living on base while my mom was a stay-at-home mother who was living a life of horror. She had an abusive marriage that no one knew of but her mother. I lived an unstable life as a child, which took me through changes as we grew up as young children. I remember her telling the story of the night she had to fight him off her after he came in drunk when she was pregnant with me. I listened to a broken heart who relived the night as she told the story of having to protect herself by embedding a butcher's knife in his forehead and hitting him with a frying pan to free herself from him. The family later moved back to Mississippi after seven years of marriage, but God had come to open the prison doors that held us captive in a bad situation.

I later became a victim of sexual abuse, which I've never spoke of to anyone, from the age of six years old until now. I remembered being woken out of my sleep in pain, but never told my mom because I was afraid and too ashamed to let anyone know, thinking I would be in trouble or bring on shame. I lost my focus dealing with something that had me feeling like I was not worthy of living.

I lived in darkness for over forty-eight years as the wave of life beat against me because of the sexual abuse in my life. I was a young lady who got married and experienced the same abuses as my mom, aunt, cousin, and friends for twenty-one years. I felt I deserved it, that it was supposed to be that way in a marriage. Even though the years passed, I became the victim of verbal and physical abuse, which started out as threats, shoving, hitting, and him actually going through with what he voiced to me he was going to do.

I conceived my second child when my firstborn was just five weeks old. I started drinking, smoking, and doing pills just to get through the nights that had me stressed out and losing my hair from what he was putting me through in the marriage. I felt I had no victory and that had me weaving from side-to-side, in and out, for most of my life. I valued the pain more than I did God and what He could do in my life. Satan was becoming more of a ruler over me than God was leading me. The enemy had my mind so messed up, fighting feelings I didn't understand, confused about love as I built up resentment toward God and men.

God had already given me sustainability in Him through His love. I had allowed my sexuality to become more to me because of what had happened when I was a child, and I felt it was the only way out of my pain. God's love was more than that of any man who claimed to love me. God's love was deeper than any pain I experienced. But I didn't know who I was in Him, and depression, unforgiveness, and discouragement ruled my heart. I allowed myself to become disconnected from God, while satan was ruling my soul, heart, and mind.

My trust issues with people grew toward those who were there to help me spiritually. The affection I looked for because I had no father in my life had me searching for something that wasn't real in my world. I was taking advantage of those I trusted and wanted to commit. At that point, I needed a prayer life that would help me disable and disengage what satan was trying to do by destroying me through his tactics.

You cannot come from being broken in the flesh into being alive spiritually if you do not know how to fight. The goal is to learn who you are in Christ, find your vision, and rest in the Father's security. My pastor once spoke on the topic, saying you should never allow your pain to become your identity, but I allowed my pain to be my weight through life (Ephesians 5:19). Satan had taken away my peace, joy, healing, and love, and death was taking control over my soul while I was running out of time with God. I couldn't fight my own battle because my spirit was dead and out of range because I was living out of order with God (Peter 2:21).

You are not born to be a leader, but you become a leader through the errors of your life. The life I lived through spiritual weakness had me broken, living with a bitter heart, and depressed (Ephesians 6:11). I had resentment toward those who were trying to help me. My heart was against what was right, and I hated myself and wanted God to end my life because I had no desire to live. I hated anyone who looked happy. I refused to take orders from my Leader who was the overseer of my soul (Job 3:21). How many long for death but it never comes because of a life you did or didn't live?

When God wants to teach you order, He will allow you to go through changes to teach you discipline. I needed to understand that it wasn't my problem that attacked me; it was satan. But God has paved the way through His death so I can have life more abundantly in Him, not my situation. I fought in my own strength. I had no prayer life and was being defeated through my bitterness and the unforgiveness that kept me from God. I didn't know how to fight what I was up against and surely didn't know how to call out when trouble arose in my life.

BREATHE
An Anthology Compiled by Melinda Walker

I was losing hope, while satan was gaining and destroying me mentally, physical, and spiritually because I had no understanding in vision, dying daily in my heart, and I had no peace. Satan was destroying me in deception, but God loved me. I had no victory and the devil was waging war in my life. I lived through pain, searching for freedom I didn't know how to get because I tried doing something God had already taken care of on that cross. I knew freedom wouldn't come by living a life that wasn't what God intended for me, thinking I was doing something right, but all the time denying the presence of evil in my life. God was looking at the heart, not the body's appearance. He wasn't looking at why I was doing wrong, but how to save myself from being destroyed by listening to the lies satan had planted inside me because of the pains I'd experienced through my life (Act 13:22).

I encourage you to exhale, *BREATHE* out, and never allow dead situations to be a dysfunction in your life and have you working improperly. His love is unconditional, and He sees what we face and go through. He has not forgotten about the hurt, pain, and suffering you have endured from others who have left you to heal yourself as if they have done no wrong. God is saying, "I call you out among the weak in faith, and to be different from those who are in darkness. I come to give life more abundantly, and love to carry you into my presence, and time for healing." He is saying, "Don't shut up heaven when the enemy comes in like a flood."

I had to exhale from all the wrong ever done in my life; for example: the lies told to me from satan to get me there at that time; my father not being in my life; man after man taking my love for granted and using me for their benefit; the ones who took advantage of me growing up; me turning away from God when I thought He left me to be stoned to death from those who had no heart; verbal abuse; physical abuse; being talked about, lied about, bullied when I was a younger age; . . . The list goes on and on. This caused so much anger inside and had me wanting to get revenge and ask, "Why?"

I encourage you to not give up on you and not to give up on ever loving again, allowing God to love you, waiting for love to be changed or moved, trusting again. Don't stop fighting. Keep pushing, pressing, and praying until God hears you. Remember, God's power and love is more than us failing. Never allow your mind to be taken where he can't grow you. Mark 8:36 says, "For what shall it profit a man, if he shall gain the whole world, and lose his soul?"

BREATHE
An Anthology Compiled by Melinda Walker

Schynies Williamson

Schynies Williamson was born on January 10, 1969, in El Paso, Texas. She has four brothers and two sisters. She is a forty-eight-year-old divorced woman with three children: Courtney, who is a police officer; Jasmine, who works with the school; and Steven Jr., who is in and out of incarceration. She also has two grandchildren, Isaiah and Traden. She has been working with the disabled for nine-and-a-half years and has been a supervisor almost a year. She has done volunteer work for daycare, Head Start schools, worked at nursing homes, cleaned houses, taken care of other people's family members, and helped her mom.

When she moved back to Mississippi at a young age, she was mostly with her grandmother (RIP) Etta Rea Jones, who taught her the value of living through God, learning to work and be a person who will lead others in life. She is looking to remarry one day. She prays for those who are going through a storm. Even at this moment, no matter what you face, God is bigger than your problem. Although you don't feel or see it, keep praising for a breakthrough to come and keep looking for favor.

Contact Schynies at:
Schynies Williamson on Facebook.com
Jasmine_ James 0923@yahoo.com

Your Past Is Necessary: Just Breathe
By: Maritza Johnson

There are things you do unconsciously that have a meaning. I was twelve years old when my life took a turn for the worst. From birth to age twelve, I thought I knew who my father was. At the age of twelve, I was taken to the Mississippi Child Support office for a DNA test. The only father I knew was no longer my father. I was conceived in a marriage but grew up in a single-parent home. I was nurtured by my older sister who was sixteen years older since my mother worked full time plus overtime hours to make ends meet. There was no male figure around, yet, when that father I knew came around, I was overwhelmed with joy.

I was always in church. My mother wouldn't allow me to miss any church services at Mt. Zion Missionary Baptist Church. I was an usher and I sang in the church choir. I was baptized at age nine. I thought this was the life and everything was how it was supposed to be. Life went on, but I didn't know my true history and didn't find out about it until I saw it spiral downward.

Age twelve was that moment when I realized I'd known my father my entire life, but never had the facts. My father was a married man who came around often. Then he became the man who was there as an every-blue-moon substitute father until age twelve. When we found out the news that DNA proved him to be my father, he slowly disappeared. Therefore, what little I did have of a father vanished.

I know many have heard of a girl trying to find her father through relationships with other men. In the summer of age fourteen, I had sex for the first time. I had my second boyfriend and thought it was love. This relationship went on for months until I found out he was cheating. I was hurt to the core because of my past, and hurtful actions with previous men and my father. I couldn't believe I had to go through this again. I couldn't believe a man could bring me down to my darkest point. I thought this man would be the key to my happiness and would mend the brokenness from my father- daughter love. My sorrow became anger, and through anger, I sought revenge. I could no longer let men take my peace and joy. I could no longer let the hurt from a man destroy me; I would need to destroy them.

At age fourteen, I became wild, sexual, and carefree. Attention-seeking would be the better way to say it. I attended a small high school in a community where mostly everyone was kin. I was beautiful, genuine, and respectful to my elders. However, deep inside there was darkness. I wanted to find my identity and overcome what I had just gone through. I lusted for attention from men. Even though I was never a dumb girl, I stopped applying myself for greatness. Whatever attention I could get, I went for.

I couldn't let what happen to me in the past from men keep me down. However, my hunger for revenge did not help me win the argument or the breakup, but I was hurt for LIFE. I removed myself from church. I became angry with God; I blamed God for all my hurt. I didn't ask to be put through this. Why did I deserve this? Why did God allow this to happen to me? This became my mentality.

I stepped out on my own, thinking I was my own God and I could handle this hurt myself. I no longer listened and meditated on the verse, 2 Chronicles 20:17, "Ye shall not need to fight in this battle: set yourself, stand ye still, and see the salvation of the Lord with you." This became irrelevant because, if He wanted to save me,

He would have never let it happen to me in the beginning. This was the worst thing I could have ever done. I took matters into my own hands.

What I didn't know was I was really just looking for love again in another man to fill my void. I had sex with over sixteen men before the age of eighteen. I thought maybe one of those men would let me in, and in return, if I gave them sex, they would love me and want to be with me, but I was wrong. I was labeled many ruthless names that would follow me the rest of my life. I didn't care if they had a girlfriend or wife, I did what I thought I needed to do to keep them. It wasn't smart, and I wasn't protecting myself while being promiscuous.

I let myself go because of heartbreaks, and I fell into darkness at age sixteen. My life took a turn for the worst I didn't think I would recover from it. I thought my life had ended, reputation had ended, and my body was no longer useful. I again blamed God, asking Him questions like: Why did You let me do this? Why did You not stop me? I asked myself the hardest question: WHO AM I?

I had no more drive, ambition, love, peace, or morals for myself. I was down to my lowest when I finally realized I had no one to turn to but God. I called out in my most-desperate and lonely hour. Reality hit me in the face: My mother was never home; my brother and I couldn't get along; I was no longer functioning intelligently in school; and I barely had a roof over my head. It seemed to be one thing after the next. I no longer felt worthy to be alive. I felt like I had no self-worth.

I had said so many disrespectful and wrong things to God that I didn't know if He would hear me even if I wanted to sneak in a prayer. I felt like I had sinned so much and had committed the ultimate sin of killing something He had given me. I felt God would turn His back on me. Yet, I was wrong. I was ready for change, I wanted to be forgiven more than anything, but I didn't know where to start. Even though I was scared to ask God, I still whispered to Him that I needed help.

I knew I had brought so much negativity to my family that they wouldn't help me. I knew I had burned so many bridges that it would be hard to build another one. I had no one else to turn to. The God I'd turned my back on before was where I had to turn back to for help. And my God had enough grace and mercy that He let me back in. I stated to Him that I didn't know the first step to take. He whispered to me, "Forgive yourself first and all those who have hurt you." It was then that I realized I had done all this because I'd never forgiven and let go of the hurt that was done to me. I asked God to guide my steps to get my life together and He did.

I started to surround myself with godly people. I started back serving and going to church, and I began to build a relationship the one Who is my Father; that was more important than any relationship. I began building a relationship with God. It came to me that it didn't matter what father or man wasn't there, God was all I needed. He is always there. He never turned His back on me. Even through my mess, He still showed me mercy and favor; it all could have been much worse. I was ashamed and didn't know how to even speak to Him. I didn't know how to reach out to Him, but He never left my side. He is my father and I am His daughter.

Everyone knows God in their own way. I was at my lowest and began to know Him there. God brought me out. God made promises to me that He kept. After I came out, I overcame my past and I forgave myself, I forgave others, and surrendered to God. I was no longer angry with my father, angry about situations, or about men because God was all I needed. Instead of letting another man mend my heart, I let God mend it. God replace the bad with love, peace, and joy. My past left me with a small package of residue. I had to build from the ground up. I had to find myself again in the Lord. Low self-esteem was an obstacle to overcome, along with generational chains and curses.

Even though so many had counted me out as no good, God counted me in to be used. He used the broken, lost, and contaminated girl. He used me to bring my family up, to break chains, and to be a model for individuals in the community. God used me to be a vessel to reach other broken people. God used me to lead my family into greatness. As a result, I became a first-generation college student, and I never imagined I would be the queen of a university. I thought perfection was what was needed for that position, but God used the imperfect girl. He used the girl with the worst past, the contaminated girl, to be the face and leader of a university. It was then I no longer let my imperfections keep me from greatness. I may have let my past go, but I didn't move forward from it until I stated I was going to be used to make a change. I was the girl who had disowned God, and yet He never left, He never gave up on me, and He still has a purpose for my life.

The voice I'd hid from singing in the church was now anointed and more useful than the times before when nothing but air would come out. The mindset of not knowing my self-worth and sleeping with unmarried and married men was no longer valid. The thoughts of staying in the "hood" and working just to make ends meet vanished. The thoughts of not believing in myself and not being smart enough went away, and I graduated from two colleges as an honor student. The thoughts of sleeping with every man, hoping they would love me, were no longer there. The thoughts of having a man to mend my heart from an absent father's love no longer exists.

My vision went from blurry to clear. Because I surrendered to God, and no longer gave myself to man, I began to have a willing spirit. It was then I found myself. When you look at me now, you can't see my past in my eyes; you see freedom. When you see me now, you feel love instead of hatred. When you see me now, you see resilience instead of bondage. When you see me now, you see JESUS.

My message to you is: Never fight your own battles. Never become a product of your environment. Never put man in the place of God. Never hold on to past hurts. God is all you will ever need. My past was necessary for who I have become today: a healed woman. Maritza K. Johnson has been set free and she has been delivered. Thank you for reading.

Maritza Johnson

Maritza Johnson is the daughter of Laretta Johnson and Raymond Butler. She is also a native of Prentiss, Mississippi, where she graduated from Prentiss High School. She is also a first-generation student. She attended undergraduate school at Mississippi Valley State University, obtaining a Social Work degree. She was also Miss Mississippi Valley State University 2013-2014. The University of Southern Mississippi is where she received a master's degree in social work. She is a licensed social worker and a Family Protection Specialist for the state of Mississippi Department of Child Protection Services. She is the second, middle, child in her mother's family.

She is a Baptist and identifies as a Christian. She is a mentor and role model in her community. She has a willing spirit, and she has surrendered to God's will and purpose for her life. She believes in having a past and not letting it define who you are. As a result of her past and what she's been through, she carries this verse in her heart: James 1: 2-3, "My brethren, count it all joy when ye fall into diverse temptations. Knowing this, that the trying of your faith worked patience."

Many Are the Afflictions of the Righteous, BUT GOD
By: Tina Watts

Growing up in Chicago was tough at times. I was the oldest of five children. With me being the oldest, I felt responsible for my sibling's safety, and I did everything I could to protect them. We fought the neighborhood children often. My activities included gathering, rocks, bricks, and sticks daily. I would tuck them safely in a pouch and hide them under the porch. We never knew when our play time would turn into a fight. I made sure we prepared ourselves for whatever the day would bring. I did have fun days where we would literally play until the sun went down. We played just as hard as we fought.

My family life took a turn in 1969. My parents separated, and we moved to New Hebron, Mississippi, to stay with my grandparents. That was a life-changing event. We went from having a bathroom in the house to an outhouse, from streetlights on every corner to complete darkness at night. It took some time for me to adjust from the city life to the country life.

After a while, we settled in and learned the life of the south. We would get out early in the morning to pick peas, butter beans, and cucumbers before school. Oh, did that take some adjusting to, but it was our new way of life. Mississippi was our new state, and my mama had made up her mind that she would not return to a life of fear. You see, my dad wasn't a good father or husband. My parents didn't have a happy marriage, so leaving was for the best.

I remember how my life changed. On September 8, 1976, I had a baby boy. He meant the world to me. He gave meaning to my life. I had responsibilities now and my life was no longer mine, but I was young, so I still wanted to experience my teenage years. On one particular day, June 3, 1978, I was invited to a house party in the neighborhood. My family was visiting me from Jackson, Mississippi. We decided to pop in for just a moment. It was my aunt, my cousins, and me. It was raining and foggy that night. When we entered the party, they had music on, and my sister, who was a great dancer, was dancing. When I looked at my sister, she had a glow over her. We said our goodbyes and headed home.

Driving home was difficult because of the fog. I was familiar with the route, but I didn't see the stop sign. I ran right into the highway. I didn't realize I was in the highway until I saw light, but it was too late. We crashed, knocking us into a service station. I remember thinking we were going to blow up because we were by a gas pump. We all were stuck in the car. It took the Jaws of Life to get my sister out. My Aunt Ava was in the front with me, and Jennifer, Roslyn, and Danielle were in the back. I lost my sister on a Monday night, but I didn't know until Wednesday. The pain of losing her still hurts.

You know, it's funny how you suppress tragic things in your life until God wants to pull things out of you. The shock and anger all wrapped up inside me was saying, "Why did you leave me? Why didn't you take me?" I had a long stay in the hospital along with my cousins. My Aunt Ava had a broken arm and was sent home. During my stay, I developed a blood clot in my lung. The doctors had to freeze my body to locate the clot. My mom was a nervous wreck. I was told she didn't want to lose me. So much of the accident I don't remember and still don't, but I do know God spared my life again. Why?

For years, I carried the burden, where I felt like I was an outcast with my family. Even though they showed love, there was still something underneath. I couldn't forgive myself. I went through life making mistake after mistake. In 1981, I moved away from home and went to stay with my cousins. I started going to church with them. I fell in love with the church we attended. There was so much love in the church and I was soaking it up. I was drowning and didn't know it. If it hadn't been for God, Who was on my side, I would have drowned in my own guilt and shame. I honestly felt like a failure and that my life did not matter.

There was a small voice that would come into my heart and tell me just the opposite. That gave me hope and gave me purpose to move forward. I didn't know what God was up to, but He had me on His mind. In 1983, I married my high school sweetheart and had two more beautiful children, a daughter and a son. I thought my life was complete. I was married with three children, working, and had a house, but I was still broken, still a hot mess. I didn't know how to be a wife and a mother.

I kept trying, but I made many mistakes. I experienced heartaches and disappointment. My husband and I came into the marriage with trust issues. He didn't trust me, and I didn't trust him. That caused our marriage to become imbalanced. We worked through the many issues we had. We remained constant because we loved each other and we loved our children, despite our many issues. I had made my mind up a long time ago that my children would be raised by their father. I knew early on that divorce hurts the children. I am a prime example of that. I didn't want that for my children. We had to come together and strike a balance. We could no longer pull in separate directions. I was determined to make my marriage work. My daughter needed her father in her life and my boys needed to know how to be a man. I couldn't do that. So, I started praying to God as He worked on me to work on my husband and He did just that. I started hungering for the Word of God.

I started going back to church and realized there was more to God than what I was getting. I started walking and met my neighbor, who later became my spiritual mother. She invited me to the church I eventually joined. I have been there ever since 1985. My transition to join another church was easy. I was criticized for joining a church that wasn't the denomination I grew up in, but nevertheless, that's where God wanted me to be spiritually fed with His Word. I have grown tremendously in the ministry. Now I am an elder in the church, ministering God's Word.

In 2001, I had a setback. We lost our home due to a fire. We lost everything. The hardest part of losing my home was losing all my memories. I lost family pictures that were so dear to me. I lost the most sentimental part of my life. I even lost the negatives from my son's wedding. That was a trying time. The pain was almost like death in the family, and we had to start completely over again. My God saw us through and now we have more now than before. I have had many turns and events in my life. Time after time God has delivered.

In 2014, the doctors found a tumor on the main artery in my neck, but thank God, it wasn't cancerous. They decided they were going to remove the tumor. The location of the tumor was a grave concern for the doctor. They wanted to run more tests before they could operate. I remember so clearly: I was in the store with my husband. I felt funny and lightheaded. My husband rushed me to the hospital. I had lost consciousness and was admitted in the hospital.

BREATHE
An Anthology Compiled by Melinda Walker

During recovery, it was detected that I'd had a stroke. I had short-term memory loss. I can remember them asking me what was my name and I did not know. I knew my husband, but none of my other family. I was lost. It was a very strange and scary time for me. I did remember to call on the Lord. God showed up and proved His Word to me again. I regained my memory. It took some time to get back what I had lost. Many are the afflictions of the righteous, but the Lord delivers them out of them all. He did it for me again. He has never failed me.

For every trial, test, and hardship I had to endure, God worked it out for my good. For every setback I encountered, and every disappointment I carried, it was for God's glory. I couldn't see it then, but now I can. God is not through with me yet. I am still a work in progress, but I am so much better since I allowed God to work on me. God is bringing wholeness in my life. He is making me a better wife and my husband a better husband. God is perfecting everything that concerns me. Now I am able to *BREATHE* again. He is the potter and I am the clay. He has the right to mold me, make me, and have His own way. It isn't about seeing the faults of others, but allowing God to work on me.

I was in need of a Savior. I was the one holding on to the past and could not release. When I let all of it go, my life changed. I met a Man named Jesus and I have not been the same.

Tina Watts

Tina Watts is married to her high school sweetheart, Willie Watts. They have been married for thirty-four years and are the proud parents of four children (one daughter and three sons) and the grandparents of eight grandchildren. She is a 1977 alumnus of Prentiss High School, and she furthered her education at several prestigious institutions such as Prentiss Institute, Jackson State University, and Jones County Junior College. She is a resident of Prentiss, Mississippi, where she is the owner of a childcare business. She has been working with children for twenty-eight years.

She is one of the elders at Outreach Fellowship Revival Center, where she is under the leadership of Pastor Jessie J. Holloway. She wears her hats in the ministry and has an opportunity to spread God's Word by WJDR, a radio station in her hometown. She assists her pastor with Sunday school when needed, ministers the Word of God, and is a leader in church choir and also over the dining committee.

Contact Tina at:

www.facebook.com/tinawatts
www.tinawatts@yahoo.com

The Eyes of God
By: Minister Niechie Baker

Picture your struggles, your downfalls, and your disappointments in the battles you've had to face and how difficult it was for you to get through them feeling misunderstood. Sometimes, like the breath was leaving your body from crying so hard, tears flowing, with no one to talk to. Full of fear, thinking the moment you opened your mouth, you would get rejected. Saying to yourself, no one will understand, and no one will believe you. So, you try to find a place to run away and hide because you think, if you can just hide and isolate yourself, maybe you can breathe.

In my life, I found many hiding places that were not healthy for me. At the ages of ten and eleven, I started to mentally run away—first thinking that my family would be better off without me. Then, one day, I physically started running away from home because I felt overlooked, misunderstood, and unloved. I was very built for my age. Around the age of twelve or thirteen, I had the physical stature of a grown woman. I recall that, during my fifth-grade year, on several occasions, older men tried to lure me into their cars while I was walking home from school. Also, in the sixth grade, a school janitor tried to convince me to have sex with him while on school grounds. Who could I turn to? I had not developed a relationship with my mother yet. I didn't feel like anybody loved me or would believe me. I was being called a fast-tail little girl by family members before I even had a chance to know what that really meant.

My life felt upside down and it caused me to rebel even more. I felt hurt and wounded with no one to talk to. All I wanted was to be loved. My upbringing wasn't perfect. There were those around me who were trying to overcome situations in their own life. My mother was the best mother she could be, but she was trying to overcome situations the enemy was using to attack her. I was too young to understand adult issues. I began to search for what I felt was lacking in my life—love in other places. I began to look for all those things outside my home. I decided to run away and connect to people I thought would love me. I will never forget it a friend of mine took me to his friend's apartment, where I thought I would be okay—only to be taken advantage of. My virginity was taken. It left me feeling lost and broken even the more. What was I going to do? I was a runaway, and he was fully aware of that fact.

After that, I was put out and left with nowhere to go. I went and sat at the bus stop, thinking, *'What am I going to do now? Surely, I can't go back home now. What will they think of me?'* I got on the Marta bus and rode to downtown Atlanta. I sat in the Marta station, hoping someone would see me and ask, "Are you okay?" or "Do you need help?" Well, this young man ended up asking me if I was okay. I never told him my age. I never told him I was a runaway because I looked grown.

He asked me, "Are you okay?"

I said, "Yeah; I just need somewhere to stay tonight."

He said, "I live with my mother, but you come over there."

So, we went to his mother's house, where I met his mother. After talking to his mother, he asked me to come to his room for a minute; he wanted to talk to me. We went to his room and he began to ask me for sex. I told him, "No." I really didn't want to have sex because of what had just happened to me. I was very lethargic because I had just been taken advantage of. I told him I wasn't up for that. I was scared, it was dark outside, and I was in the middle of nowhere. But, so I wouldn't be put out, I slept with him. I will never forget it: I just lay there—no emotion, no sound, no feeling—crying on the inside. At this point, I wanted to go just home, but I still was afraid.

I knew I was a runaway and I hadn't been going to school; therefore, I knew, by now, the police were looking for me, and when they caught me, I would be arrested. I didn't want to get locked up, so I kept running until I couldn't run any more. Finally, I showed up at home. Things didn't feel the same. I felt like I didn't belong. I felt like the street was my home. I tried to go back to school, but I would always end up fighting and being lied on, so I ran again. I went back to that same place, thinking, *'If only I could talk to his mother about what's going on with me, perhaps she'll understand and help me by allowing me to stay there that night.'* Only to find out after I did, I had given the enemy more power to really try to destroy me.

After her son overheard our conversation, he told me to, "Come here." As I told him what was going on with me, he started touching on me. I told him to "Stop!", but he forced himself on top of me to have sex with me. I continued to say, "NO! STOP!" He cursed me out, then beat me while having sex. I started screaming for his mother, but she didn't say a word. This man was crazy; his mother was afraid of him because she had no control over him. He finally got off me, and when I tried to get out the house, the door was locked. I looked at his mother and asked, "Can you let me out?" She didn't say a word, and finally again, he cursed me out, but he let me go. I never looked back, but I didn't go back home either.

I start hanging out in areas where drug dealers and prostitutes were because I knew they stayed up all night long, and if hung around them, they would invite me everywhere they went. Many times, I was hungry, with nowhere to lay my head and nowhere to go. I was exposed to so many things. I walked around wondering why did I feel like no one loved me or no one wanted me.

The last time I'd even felt the expression of love was when my grandmother and grandfather were living. I felt like my mother loved me, but it was hard for me to feel the love. I was raised in a home with my grandfather, grandmother, mother, sister, brother, uncle, aunt, and three cousins. My grandfather was a minister and he showed me what the image of a godly man should be. When he died, a piece of me started to fade, and the streets of Atlanta showed me something different about men, which disgusted me. The image of what I thought was a man was gone. I hated men at this point. I was really trying to find a way to breathe because life itself had made it difficult for me to breath. I spent countless days and nights on the streets of Atlanta with nowhere to go. I thought about my family every day, but because of what happened to me on those streets, I didn't want to go home and contaminate my family with the things I had encountered.

I processed some things in my mind at an early age, thinking it was better for me to stay away from my family than to be with them and bring them grief. I felt that staying away would be better. Actually, it wasn't, but that was how I processed it at that time. While I was a runaway, I ended up getting ill while I was staying at a hotel with this lady. There were flyers posted everywhere with my pictures on them; they were on telephone poles everywhere. I didn't know that someone at the hotel had seen my face on a flyer. They called the police. The police and my mother showed up. They locked me up, and I spent time in juvenile before they sent me home on restriction.

BREATHE
An Anthology Compiled by Melinda Walker

My mother took me to the clinic to get me checked because I had been in the streets for a long time. I remember it like it was yesterday. I overheard my mother on the phone; she was crying and she looked devastated. The next day my auntie came over to our house. My mother was lying in bed and looked torn. My auntie said, "Come here, Niechie; I want to talk to you." Then she said, "You're pregnant, and it's your choice to keep it or you can have an abortion." I didn't know what to do at the time. I didn't even look pregnant. I was terrified. I knew who my baby father was because before I was found at the hotel, I had been living with a woman in the Perry homes where he lived also. She took me in for a long time until she found out I was a runaway. She had a talk with me and I left; that was how I ended up at the hotel.

With that news, I felt like I was stuck with having to make the worst decision of my life. At the time though, I thought it was the best decision for me because I was only a child and I agreed to have an abortion. Right before the abortion took place, they told me I was six months pregnant and that it was a baby boy. The abortion took place in a small country town in Georgia. After the abortion, I stayed home only for a little while. When I went back to the doctor for a checkup after the abortion, they ran tests. Weeks later, a letter came in the mail to my mother from the teen clinic. I opened the mail and read it without my mother knowing the mail had come. The letter horrified me! It stated I had something called dysplasia. After reading the letter, it sounded life-threatening. Instantly, I panicked. I wrote a letter and told my mother I was on drugs and I couldn't stay. I left the letter on the bed, so when she woke up to look for me, she would read it and know why I was not there. I wanted to make her feel like that was why I was running away. At that point, I felt useless. I felt like I was about to die and I felt couldn't stay. I jumped out of the window. I was afraid.

BREATHE
An Anthology Compiled by Melinda Walker

I ran for months. They caught me again and placed me into state custody, where it was terrible. I ended up in numerous treatment centers, where I witnessed girls raping girls with deodorant bottles, and instructors were flirting with the girls in the facility. On one occasion, I remember being dragged, put in a straitjacket naked, and needles being stuck in my side. Some of the treatment centers I was placed in were not the best, but that's what the state was offering at the time. In my process, I reached the age of sixteen and I maxed-out my time at state treatment centers. I was sent home, still full of pain and hurt, thinking of all the things that had happened to me while I was on the streets and in my home.

By this time, I was furious and mad with my mother and father. I began to rebel and my heart became hard. I tried to finish high school, but my mind was so consumed with my failures in life, I couldn't focus in school. Eventually, I dropped out and started living a life full of foolishness. I got two jobs, and all I did was stack money and club. I started to look at men differently, I felt men were disgusting. I started to hang out with those who live alternative lifestyles—homosexuality.

I loved them, but I didn't like what they were doing. I hated the act of homosexuality because, at a young age, one of my childhood, older female neighbors molested me under the house while we were playing hide and seek. I was angry; she did it for a long time. I didn't realize my hanging around that spirit when I got older was going to open a stronger demonic door in my life that would lead to other demons. I started to be attractive to women. I began to like the girls who dressed like boys.

That spirit began to consume me and I started to enter another level of perversion. I started sleeping with women, not realizing I had encountered demonic soul ties when I was a runaway. After a while, I learned how to master the women. I studied them, I learned what they liked, and I knew how to get their attention. If they were struggling in their minds, I already knew that struggle. At that time, satan was using and preparing me to destroy countless women's lives. I would wait on opportunities to gain the trust of the women, only to leave them in a broken and desolate place. I did not care if it took three months, six months, one or two years; I was assigned to get them converted to become a lesbian. I waited for things in their life to surface, like broken relationships, broken marriages, financial needs, or a woman being in a vulnerable state. That's how the enemy used me to creep in.

I learned how to get in a woman's mind, and after mastering the lifestyle, I only dealt with women who never thought about being a lesbian, and those who were struggling and wanted to try it out. I never really looked for those who were openly gay until after some time of being in the lifestyle. In my single time, I did a lot of game playing. I didn't want the women and I had no desire to sleep with them, but I found excitement in playing a part in getting them converted over. They would beg me to turn them out, but that wasn't my assignment in the kingdom of darkness. I was only to get them converted over.

With this demonic spirit of perversion, came lying, stealing, disobedience, deceit, gossip, and so many more things. I was operating in a lying spirit and a spirit of deceit. Satan is deceitful, and his assignment is to kill, steal, and destroy. As I lived this lesbian lifestyle, I felt there was nothing wrong with it. I lived it publicly. I wasn't ashamed! I believed God was okay with me being gay because God is a God of love. Surely nothing would happen to me because I dated a woman. I never thought I'd gotten into lesbianism because I was molested as child or because I'd started hanging in environment full of homosexuality.

I got in a long-term relationship with a woman that lasted almost ten years. In that relationship, God used this young lady to bring me back to Him. Funny isn't it? Why would your ex-lover take you back to God, knowing, if you found Jesus for real, the relationship would be over? Well, because it was all in God's plan for me to know Him for real. He said in His Word, I am the apple of His eye, not realizing the eyes of God were always on me.

It was evident that He lived in her and was speaking to her as well. During a lot of my lesbian years, I lived in the state of Tennessee. When I started this lifestyle, I was living in state of Georgia. Eventually, I told my mother I was gay and all she ever spoke was, "Niechie, God knows your address." I didn't understand at that time, but later I did. She did not bash me, she did not put me down, she just spoke those words to me. By this time in my mother's life, she had really developed a strong relationship with the Lord and was being led by the Holy Spirit. Her life consisted of praying, studying, worshiping, and seeking the Lord. As time went by, I told my sister the same thing I had told my mother—that I was gay—and she said, "Niechie, no you're not." At that time, I didn't understand the power of words, I really didn't understand, but my sister was speaking me out of a situation

I can recall one night, I started to have sex with my ex-lover. I began to cry and scream out the name of Jesus right in the middle of it, not realizing or thinking about what my mother had meant when she said, "God knows your address." Jesus meet me right there in the middle of my mess. He came right to my address and began to work on me. I began to give my life over to Him, and through the Holy Spirit, He began to deliver me from the things that were causing me to feel as if I could not breathe. The Holy Spirit came in my life and begin to manifest Himself, and I began to *breathe* again. He gave me a new way of walking, a new way of talking, a new way of thinking, and new way of living. Thank God for being born again. The Holy Spirit transformed my mind.

One key to my transformation was isolation from the things that had me bound. Another key to my transformation was staying consistently in His Word, and trusting and believing in His Word. Another main key was obeying the Word. The Bible says, "Obedience is better than sacrifice" (1 Samuel 15:22). The Holy Spirit taught me that living a yielded, submitted life will keep me fine-tuned with the things of the Spirit. He also taught that, when you don't yield and submit to Him, it will spiritually suffocate you, and you won't be able to reap the life of abundance. By following what the Holy Spirit taught me, Jesus delivered me from a lot of things that had me bound.

I want you to know you can be free as well. No matter what your struggles are, Jesus is the answer, and He is your only Lifeline. He is the only way, the only breath that has the power to heal, set free, and deliver. It is Jesus! I want to leave you with this: God Word is true, and He says He will never leave you or forsake you. In my life, I didn't understand that the eyes of God were keeping me, protecting me, and preserving me. He never left me during any time in my life. It may have looked like it, it may have felt like it, but when I got an understanding of His Word, I came to grips with He was always there and I was in a spiritual battle—good fighting evil. I found out good overrides evil and I found out that that Good is Jesus!! *Jesus paid it all* for every sin I committed, or any sin committed against me. I found out that at the cross, Jesus found no fault in me. There was forgiveness for me at the cross, there was healing at the cross, there was love at the cross, and there was deliverance at the cross for me. I found out that every demon that had tried to plague my life, the blood of Jesus and the power of the cross had destroyed them all.

Now let us pray. Father, in the name of Jesus, I thank You that whoever reads this, their life will never be the same. Holy Spirit, dismantle every demonic attachment the enemy has assigned to their life. Spirit of Truth, begin to expose every lie and every spirit that has come to kill, steal, and destroy. Father, in the name of Jesus, we command every soul tie, every generational curse, and lying spirit to be severed in the spirit, now in Jesus' name.

Now, fire of the Holy Ghost be upon their body. Father, in Jesus' name, loose their mind. Satan, come out of their heart, come out of every area that was entered through disobedience, through childbirth, through molestation and rape, through TV, through music, through incest, through pictures, through radio, through tattoos, through ungodly sacrifices. We command you to come up by the roots and leave their body, now in the Mighty Name of Jesus.

Now, Mighty Counselor, Spirit of Truth, we ask You to awaken their spirit man and cause them to be sober and alert. Sharpen their discernment now, in Jesus' name. I speak life into them and life more abundantly, as Jesus has already spoken. Now transform their mind, causing their mind to be a Christ-like mind. Fill them with the fruit of the Spirit: love, joy, peace, patience, kindness, goodness, faithfulness, gentleness, and self-control. I speak that they will have the power to stand on the Word of God, and when the enemy comes and tries to remind them who they used to be, they will let him know who they are today. They are a warrior priesthood, a chosen generation. Now, Holy Spirit, *increase revelation, increase knowledge, and increase supernatural power, in Jesus' name. Amen!*

The Word of God says He neither slumbers or sleeps. His eyes roam to and forth throughout the earth. He said no man can pluck you out His hand. Remember, you are the apple of His eye and the eyes of God are always on the faces of His beloved.

Minister Niechie Baker

Minister Niechie Baker is a prophetic chosen vessel and visionary of the Kingdom of God. She is the mother of three. She was born and raised in Atlanta, Georgia. She traveled extensively to spread the Gospel of Jesus Christ. She operates in the fivefold ministry. She is anointed and appointed to set the captives free. Her Outreach Ministry is You Can Change Ministries, YCCM. It is evident that she has a passion to win souls for Christ and is equipped to save the loss at any cost by reaching out to men and women, boys and girls, who are struggling with dysfunctional lifestyle. She lives by John 3:16: "For God so loved the world that He gave his one and only Son, that whoever believes in Him shall not perish but have eternal life."

She is not afraid to tell how her mess became a message, her test turned into a testimony, and her trials into tryouts. Her favorite quote is locked and loaded with the Holy Ghost, and is one of the best ammunitions anybody can possess. She is determined to be a voice crying out in the wilderness, preparing the people for the return of Jesus Christ, so they will reap the reward of His promises, which is eternal life with Him.

Contact Minister Niechie Baker at:

Facebook: Niechie Baker
Email: niechieb@gmail.com

How God's C.P.R. Restored my Spiritual Pulse: The Resuscitation

By: Gwendolyn Braswell-Burkes

What do you do when you are out of breath, gasping for the very breath that is vital to your very soul? When life itself seems to be running away from you and spiritual unconsciousness has invaded the very fibers of your being? The air blockage has crushed you and ushered you to a place where you begin drowning in your own blood?

That was me so many years ago, a period where the breathing seemed impossible. I was drowning in deeper waters. The more I tried to breathe, the more intense the troubles of life began to suffocate everything that was put in me to survive. I had become a nomad, going from place to place, never finding the fresh airways to relieve this breathing dysfunction. It ignited a slow process, as if someone had added dead weight to me. The hurt of it pulled me all the way to the bottom.

Just like the words of John 10:10, the thief's desire was to "steal, kill, and destroy" my destiny. That was a season where my lifeline had been stolen, with a personal agenda to kill me and destroy my destiny. Satan was surely on his job, but soon he was about to become unemployed! In a world of mere uncertainty, I felt invisible. I was blinded by the enemy's agenda. There I was, wandering to and fro in the natural world with a spiritual ball and chain. Its mission accompanied me into the deep, dark blue seas of this life. Satan thought his mission was accomplished!

So, there I sat, all the way at rock bottom, and I couldn't figure out how to get back up. Spiritually, I was flat-lining. My eyes could see, but my mind was in a state of shock. Toiling in those waters with nowhere to go, I felt deserted with the bleeding wounds of hurt and abuse. Suffering in the silence of mental, physical, and emotional torment became a residence that covered the echoes of my inward screams. No one heard the cries of my heart. It was like I was stranded on a deserted island. Yes, I was stuck in those waters, and no one could see or hear me. The abandonment pushed my pain to become numb. I was just looking, but not seeking, not a word to revive me nor an answer to sustain me.

Suddenly, I got the strength to look up. There was a beautiful light above that mesmerized me, and a long arm stretched out, reached toward me, and pulled me to shore. Then, He removed the ball and chain. But I still wasn't breathing and could barely move.

Then I heard a phrase in my spirit that connected me with a spiritual responder: "C.P.R. is needed." Instantly, I awakened to a moment of confusion. I heard, "She is going to be okay. Keep a close eye on her." And someone else said, "Yes, Dr. Kena!"

The confusion got a little intense. There were missing pieces that I was trying to put together. How did I get here? There was a lady with a beautiful smile on her face just looking at me. My memory began to resurface. Yes, the kids were at their grandmother's house for the weekend. She told me her name was Nurse Anna, and she offered her assistance of accommodation if I needed anything. I felt so comfortable around her. She began to explain how I'd gotten there. She told me I had been walking in terrible stormy weather, and a Good Samaritan had brought me to the emergency room. She added that from the ER, I'd ended up in Behavioral Health.

Finally, I clearly remembered what happened. Jaylon and I had gotten into an argument. The feelings overloaded my thoughts, which geared my focus off everything that mattered in my life. The abuse and disrespect brought a heavy blow to my emotional capacity. The life in me was slowly draining. Every breath got weaker. The cross I had to bear got heavier as I tried to balance it on this seesaw of life. Jaylon couldn't be trusted any more. He blew every wind of my hope away from me, almost like a sucker punch because I never saw it coming.

There I was in my own valley of dry bones. Insecurity and low self-esteem seemed to have choked the very breath out of me. The repetitive cheating and discovering drugs in my drinks pushed me closer to the edge. Then he did the unthinkable: he slept with my boss. Upon reflection, I now understood the everyday tension in the office each day as I would gasp for air. Thinking of how hard I worked to make my boss look good, I got very angry.

Then I took deep breaths, and a calmness overcame me. I heard that loving voice again that said, "C.P.R. is needed." This began to be the wind that blew me out of my valley of dry bones. I began to read my Word more often, and as a result, I ran into one of the most beautiful love letters from God. Ezekiel 16:6: "And when I passed by you and saw you drowning in your blood, I said to you in your blood, Live! Yes, I said to you, Live!" This Word was the beginning of my recovery to effectively *BREATHE* again. My sight became clearer as I realized my worth. I saw myself as my Father saw me. The fog was clearing as the process began to revive my lifeless situation. The revelation became clear that I was breathing in a toxic environment which was truly hazardous to my health. The remedy involved me digging deep into my spiritual roots. This was a spiritual emergency and I wanted to live!

The beginning phase was C-Change. Yes, change was instrumental in the resuscitation. God reminded that His Word kept me grounded. I had to find my way back to Jesus. Ezekiel 16:6 brought about a spiritual awakening in me. It resurrected me out of a puddle of my own mess. God saw me drowning in my own mess, and He said, "Live!"

That one word empowered me to help myself. I began to attend support groups required to help me through my near-spiritual-death experience. It ignited my spirituality to another level. Change was definitely the key, but transformation was the fuel that shifted me into breathing without spiritual inhalers. I began breathing on my own. No longer did I have to hold on to someone's shirt tail.

As transformation steered me in the right direction, it pushed me to the second phase of P-Position. Positioning myself was indeed the fresh new wind to my healing. Without breathing on my own, how could I stand on my own? As the oxygen came to my brain, God renewed my mind. The blood of Jesus circulated in my spiritual body, flowing freely in and through me. This blood transfusion diffused all the toxins of the hurt and pain. The positioning phase required a strong prayer life. He revealed the mistakes I'd made through ineffective decision-making as well as a minimal prayer life.

BREATHE
An Anthology Compiled by Melinda Walker

The more I became positioned, the stronger I was able to stand. I knew my identity as my Father saw me. This new relationship rekindled the emptiness I was longing for.

Why didn't I realize that no man should make me get to a point of wanting to end my life and leave my children? How could I have gotten so low that I would walk four miles in a storm? Nobody but God can get you through such an ordeal! Positioning got even easier. I was like a babe in Christ who learned how to digest the words which strengthened my legs to walk alone without a spiritual life alert. No longer did I need a panic button to push a button every time I fell down. Like David, I encouraged myself! One minute, I was barely standing, but I learned how to persevere through every obstacle I encountered. No more rescue breaths for me. I'd received the breath of life!

The last part of this process played a vital role to my true healing. It was not easy, but necessary to live a life of total transformation. Release was definitely essential in this process. One thing I realized about this final phase of C.P.R. is you can't truly *BREATHE* until you R-RELEASE! You have to exhale to release that spiritual carbon dioxide—what is not good for you. In the past, I never made it to the release process because I was trying to do it on my own. Going through the full process kept me from becoming spiritually unconscious all over again.

I realized I had to release what had hurt me in my past. Forgiving everyone who'd hurt me brought deliverance and activated my breathing. I had to loosen the soul ties that kept me returning to the same relationship. So much had remained heavy on my heart until I couldn't breathe fresh air.

That's why I nearly flatlined every time. We have to realize there is only one true Savior. Normally, I wouldn't make it through the process, but God yelled "CLEAR!" He said "LIVE!" and I did just that! The Great Physician gave me His clearance to return to my work that He has called me to do. In spite of the molestation, abuse, and soul ties, I learned to let go. This phase was hard but necessary to breathing. For so many years, I didn't speak to people because I didn't forgive. I took off the spirit of heaviness and put on a garment of praise. All the heaviness disappeared off my chest. My spiritual air passage is now unclogged!

Not repenting was an accomplice to me not truly being delivered to breathe freely. I had to follow up with my heavenly Father for checkups as I examined myself daily. This time, the process was successful. I left Jaylon and mastered the process. Moving to a new city pushed me into my purpose. My Savior freed me, and I even got married. My husband later passed in 2015, but he loved me through thick and thin. We birthed an awesome ministry together, and our ministry is still breathing!

The love of my Savior made it all possible. I fell in love with my Hero. As the Master of the sea heard my despairing cry, He lifted me from the deepest, darkest place in my life. I laid aside every weight. God unlocked the shackles as He pulled the keys out of MY pocket. Yes, He's given US the keys, and as I pulled them out in those drowning waters of pity, shame, abuse, and bondage, those keys were a perfect fit to my breathing. God is my doorkeeper and locksmith. I survived, and my head is now above water. Breathing and now unstoppable, my spiritual pulse is now restored!

BREATHE
An Anthology Compiled by Melinda Walker

Gwendolyn Braswell-Burkes

Gwendolyn Braswell-Burkes is a true soldier for Christ. She was born June 7, 1974, in Albany, Georgia. She is a graduate of Westover Comprehensive High School. Through the ups and downs of life, she has been a driving force to empower others to excel to their fullest potential in her community. She is the co-founder of Dry Bones Street Project. This ministry was started in 2010 along with her late husband Arthur Burkes. Through their vision, many lives have been changed and empowered. Many programs were birthed to empower individuals to self-sufficiency. Projects include: H.E. Program, S.H.E. Program, BABES program, and the Diva-Fella ball, which is for GED graduates.

Her project, Lighten the Load, is a tool she uses to evangelize in the laundromats to the lost. Gwen is always thinking of innovative ways to continue to win souls to Christ through writing plays and songs. She is an Evangelist and serves on the Praise and Worship and Intercessory Teams at Grace Community Church, where Frederick Caldwell is her pastor. Through this project, the youth will learn how to do the work of an Evangelist through acting, singing, and writing. They will also learn how to implement their own projects as the gifts are stirred up in a new generation of future leaders of tomorrow. Gwen also has a passion for women who have been hurt and broken. She works with women of domestic violence as she is a fifteen-year survivor of abuse.

Gwen is on a continued mission to promote transformation. She feels transformation is a deeper accountability for change. Through conferences, seminars, and other projects, her hope is that transformation will supersede change.

Gwendolyn is the mother of three beautiful children: Jamarcus, Jacobi, and Jameshia. She resides in the Atlanta area with her beautiful family. She will not stop until she fulfills the purpose and calling God has placed on her life. Gwen will continue to take leaps and bounds to do the work of an Evangelist and to continue the great commission God has placed on her life.

Contact Gwendolyn Braswell at:

Facebook: https://www.facebook.com/gwendolyn.braswell
Email: Gwendolyn.Braswell@yahoo.com

Surrendering in the Storms of Life
By: Jennifer L. May

As I began to write this chapter, I realized I could only birth my chapter as the Holy Spirit moved me, and only say what God had given me to say. For weeks, I have walked to and fro, seeking God for direction. Waiting has taught me I can't have it my way, but God's way. The birthing has been difficult and even painful. Many nights I've gone to bed crying, and I have risen in the early morning crying because of the thoughts that intruded on my mind. So, as you read this chapter, know that this is a work of the Spirit. God is breathing a message through His daughter for a time such as this.

As a child, my life was grand. I'm the middle child of three and the only girl. My brothers loved me, but often called me bossy. Most of my life has revolved around family and church. My mom's ultimate goal was to see her husband and children saved, therefore, I've held close to what is true and that's the Word of God. My mom was, and still is, the spiritual glue that holds our family together. She knows we need God to make it.

I accepted the Lord as my personal Savior at an early age. My former pastor's wife was very adamant about children falling in love with Jesus while they were young. Although I didn't fully understand everything about salvation, I gladly surrendered my life to God. Surrendering is one of the best decisions I could have ever made.

At the age of twelve years old, I gave my life to the Lord. I was doing all the things people told me to do, yet still a child. I never forgot I was only twelve years old, but they did. I cannot tell you it was easy because it was not. The peer pressure that derived from it was almost unbearable. There were times when there were people to encourage me, but there were also times I felt as if I was walking this Christian journey all alone. Then one day, I became a teenager.

Life took a turn for the worst. First of all, I had a very strong personality. I am also an alpha female. As a teenager, I was fighting against my very own nature, the core of who I am. I had to learn how to love me and embrace who I was. I was a teenager looking like an adult. On many occasions, I was pursued by older men. At that time, I thought it was cute and so did my friends. It was not until I was violated at the age of fifteen that I came to the realization that it was not cute. My heart was broken, my faith shaken, and my life shattered. The element of fear sat in, and so did anger, bitterness, and retaliation.

Then it became "matters of the heart". I began struggling in my own way, trying to do what was right from my heart. As people, our lives have been constructed by the laws of intellect. We are programmed by, "If you do me wrong," my intellect reacts and says, "I am going to do you wrong." My brain began to teach me how to scheme, lie, connive, and manipulate. I was so hurt and my life was in such a mess that all of those things felt right. But God put a spirit of conviction in my heart that corrected me when I did wrong and that conviction is still in my heart today.

For many years, this plagued me. My life was tormented by this very act. Lies and rumors surfaced and caused my family so much pain. I began blaming myself and started to hate me. Although it seemed as if I was winning in the public eye, I felt like a loser. My walk with Christ became stagnated. Not only did I disconnect from God, but I had a social disconnect with people. I became insecure and secluded. I was moved by emotions through my logical mind which made me only look out for number one, and that was me. It's a reality that emotions and logic react to "threats" they perceive around them. It makes it seem as though everyone else is always wrong.

At some point, I realized my life was in a downhill spiral. I gave birth to a beautiful baby boy, married at a young age, and three children were born to that union. For many years, I bounced in and out of church, doing things my way. My emotions were never intact, and the least little thing sent me over the edge. I had lost touch with the Master.

On December 25, 1999, I was traveling along Highway 13 North from Silver Creek, Mississippi, to Magee, Mississippi, where I resided at the time. My two-month-old daughter Amber and I were asleep in the front seat while her father was driving and suddenly fell asleep. The car drove straight off the cliff, causing the point of impact to be deadly. This tragic accident claimed the life of my daughter on Christmas night, causing our lives to never be the same again. I suffered many injuries, along with head trauma that resulted in me being in a coma for several days. God was definitely in control.

After coming out the coma, I had to get into motion to face what had happened. Learning about the death of my daughter sent me into a long and difficult grief journey that no parent can ever be prepared to take. The first year after Amber's death was pure torture. Every time someone smiled at me, I thought they were laughing at me. I became severely depressed. Amber's death took my breath away. I would cry and scream out in the middle of the night, causing my parents to nearly have a heart attack. At first, I lived from second to second, not knowing what the next minute was going to bring.

Amber's death was so unnatural, and I found myself always fighting that unnaturalness. I began to feel a state of numbness trying to allow my emotions to catch up with what my mind was telling me. The numbness and disbelief helped to insulate me from the reality of the death of my baby girl. My marriage failed after many years of trying to cope. He blamed himself and felt as though I blamed him as well because I was never happy. We separated, but at some point, we learned we could be friends. I thought I would never laugh again, but there I was a year later, laughing.

My family and friends embraced me through this difficult time in my life and God encamped His angels all around me. I had a great spiritual support system. My most memorable encounter with God after the accident was when I attended one of Bishop T.D. Jakes' conferences in Atlanta, Georgia. Through him, I've learned I can't allow life to get me down. I had to pursue my calling by discovering my purpose. I realized to do this, I must purify myself. I needed to engage myself in prayer. I needed a new heart.

God began to do a heart transplant on me right there in the middle of the conference. Hallelujah! I surrendered my all to Him with outstretched hands. My life was no longer my own. I needed God to touch me so that I could *BREATHE*. All God asks is that when we pray, He wants us to believe in Him and His promises.

When I returned to Mississippi, my prayer life had changed. I had a new walk, a new talk, and a new look. I learned that prayer embraces the smallest things in life. It reaches to everything that concerns a man or woman, whether it be their body, hearts, minds, or souls. I believed, "The effectual fervent prayers of a righteous man availeth much" (James 5:16). I was reconnected to God!

BREATHE
An Anthology Compiled by Melinda Walker

At that point, I was on a roll. I was back in church, serving God, and fulfilling my purpose. During that time, I faced some challenges, but that's life. I've always been a person to overcome every obstacle I've been faced with. One of my favorite scriptures states, "For I know the plans I have for you, declares the Lord, plans to prosper you and not to harm you, plans to give you a hope and a future" (Jeremiah 29:11 NIV). I believe that for me and my children.

Journeying through life, we faced many challenges and disappointments. I experienced an abusive marriage that almost cost me my life. I knew I needed to be free from the terrible bondage that entrapped me. I remained in the marriage for many different reasons. I felt I needed him to face the destructive nature of his behavior and to give him an opportunity to seek spiritual help. When there was no change, I knew then it was hopeless without God. This had been a long and difficult journey, and I needed to find healing for the children and myself. I soon left the marriage and divorced him. However, I continued to trust God throughout the process.

I became angry. Despite all I went through, I embraced the journey and sought God for help to face what lay ahead. I trusted God to provide the necessary elements I needed to rebuild a strong foundation, but I had to be willing to embrace the road ahead. I knew the joy of the Lord was my strength and there is nothing too hard for Him.

As I continued to journey through life, I remarried, and he was the apple of my eye. This man was a God-fearing man who loved the Lord. He was the epitome of a man seeking after God's own heart. I loved him with every fiber of my being. We were married for only two years. During our first year of marriage, he was working offshore and suddenly became ill. He was later diagnosed with congestive heart failure. My faith was so strong in the Lord that I believed God for a new heart. First of all, God had already done a spiritual heart transplant on me, so why couldn't He give my husband a physical heart transplant? We were in out and out of hospitals all the time, but continuing to trust God.

One year later, he was placed on the list for a heart transplant, but he died months later. July 22, 2014, took my breath away. Yet again, I had lost someone who was so dear to me. I didn't question the Lord because He had already prepared me for such a time as this. I had begged God to heal my husband time and time again. I was able to plan his funeral, handle our financial affairs, and prepare to return to work without losing my mind. Many thought I didn't take the time to go through the grieving process. The fact of the matter is, I was afraid to. I knew God had completed a work in my husband that no one else could do.

With that being said, God had done just what I'd asked Him to do. Many didn't understand it, but I did. God healed him; He just healed him on the other side. What felt like death to other family members begin to feel like life to me. Why? It was because I was to my husband who I was supposed to be to him, when I was supposed to be. I honored my husband and my marriage. I served him with diligence and grace, and God granted me a peace that surpassed all understanding.

Through all the tragedies in life, God turned my tragedies into triumphs and my woes into wows! I was shattered but not broken, wounded but now I'm healed! God rescued me and now I can *BREATHE*. I wouldn't take anything for my journey now. In Christ, I am wiser and stronger than I've ever been. The devil came to kill, steal, and destroy me, but God came that I may have life and have it more abundantly. I have life and I have it more abundantly.

BREATHE
An Anthology Compiled by Melinda Walker

In conclusion, I count it all joy! I'm a winner in Christ Jesus. I have a daughter and a husband who have gone on to be with the Lord. They are walking streets that are paved with gold. No more suffering, no more crying, they have gone to be with the King. I know if I live the life Christ wants me to, I will one day see them again. Although I suffered a great deal, God delivered me out of it all! He rescued me and now I can *BREATHE*.

Jennifer L. May

Jennifer L. May was born in Jefferson Davis County, but raised in Silver Creek, Mississippi. She is the daughter of Mr. Elijah and Mary Barnes. She is the middle child of three children and the only girl. She was recently united in holy matrimony to Mr. Andrew May, and they proudly share three sons, a daughter, two beautiful granddaughters, and a daughter-in-law in this union.

She is a lifelong member of Lucas Tabernacle Church of Christ Holiness U.S.A., under the leadership of Elder Rufus Fields, where she serves in many different capacities. She is currently the correspondence secretary, president of the Inspirational Choir, vice president of the United Christian Women's Ministries, parliamentarian of the Youth Ministry, and district facilitator of L.I.F.T., Ladies in Fellowship Together.

Jennifer graduated from Lawrence County High School in May of 1995 and completed her Bachelor of Science Degree in Psychology from William Carey University in August 2012. She is currently employed with the Mississippi Department of Rehabilitation Services as a counselor and is pursuing a master's degree in Rehabilitation Counseling. She is a firm believer that positive actions, combined with positive thinking, results in success! "I can do all things through Christ who strengthens me."

Contact Jennifer L. May at:

@jennifer.hawthorne.338
Jenniferwinfield03@yahoo.com
601-455-9904

Overcoming the Impossible by God's Grace
By: Demetre Francis

It is possible to overcome the impossible by God's grace and His great mercy. After all I have been through, I now can *BREATHE*.

I was the only girl in my family, and that was very hard. I was always a heavy, dark-skinned girl, and I felt I was ugly. I grew up with very low self-esteem and I always distanced myself from everyone. I didn't have any friends and I kept to myself. I struggled daily with loving and accepting myself for who God created me to be. My life as a youth was very stressful. Many days I wanted to give up on life. In my high school days, I started acting out. I was full of anger because I didn't feel I fit in. I hated school because I had to interact with people. In my eleventh grade year, I got kicked out. It was then me against the world. I really suffered and fell into a deep depression. I had no education, and I was lonely and unhappy. I felt that my life was pointless.

I often reflect on what might life might have been like if my father had been in my life to protect me. I had a big void in my life. My dad just appeared after years of not being there. I decided to try to have a relationship with him. He continued to come around, and I began to let my guards down and kind of trust him. Time progressed . . . then it happened: my breath was taken, and the enemy came in and destroyed my life. The man who was there to protect me, violated me. He didn't sexually assault me once, but twice! I was devastated. I was hurt to the core. I felt so dirty and uncomfortable with myself. I lost trust in all men. At that point, I no longer wanted to live. I had no excitement about my future. Everything was pointless. I felt so unworthy. I cried night and day. I began to blame myself and started hating who I was.

My life became unbearable until God sent two godly, wonderful people into my life: my pastor, Jessie Holloway, and Barbara Holloway. They introduced me to a Man named Jesus. They led me through the plan for salvation. Roman 10:9 states, "If I will confess with my mouth the Lord Jesus and believe in my heart that God has raised Him from the dead, I will be saved." I began to pray and read my Bible. My relationship with the Lord began to grow. I started to know God for myself. When I didn't understand certain things, my pastor and first lady would always take time out to help me grasp and understand. I started to feel good about myself. My self-esteem improved. I started believing God loved me just like I am. I started encouraging myself, speaking God's Word over myself. I would spend hours in my room, studying and praying. I began attending services regularly and surrounding myself with church family for strength. I was able to *BREATHE*. I held my head up. I found my peace and joy in the love of God. I began to live through the eyes of God. God brought me out of that low place. I came out of that comfort zone of being an introvert. I started getting out more, surrounding myself with people.

I stayed afloat for some years, but as time progressed, I let my guards down, and slowly, I allowed the enemy back into my life. All the hard work I'd done to get my life back was slowly dwindling. I slowly stopped praying and reading my word. I found myself back in the same place I was. I stopped going to church and I backslid into my old ways. It got worse and worse. I started drinking and partying. I met this guy who told me everything I wanted to hear. I got pregnant and our relationship started going downhill. The relationship became unhealthy, but I was blinded by crazy love. I was pregnant, so I wanted the relationship to work. After realizing he wasn't the one for me, I had to let the relationship go. This was a very hard thing to do.

I started back praying daily, but nothing happened. I felt like God had closed His ears to my prayers. I stressed so much until I had an early delivery. My daughter was born at two pounds, three ounces. She had to stay in the hospital for two weeks. Now I had a premature baby with no job, money, or car. I was ashamed. I wanted to go back to church, but for fear of how I thought they'd see me, I didn't. I really became depressed. I felt like I'd failed God and that I could never get back my relationship with Him. The enemy started working on my mind, and one day, I took a lot of pills. I wanted to end it all, but God had a plan for my life. The enemy came to steal my life, but God allowed me to live. I wanted God to help me out of this or let me die. He told me, "I came to give you life and life more abundantly."

My pastor and first lady were there when I woke up. They stood with me and prayed for me. They ministered God's Word to me and encouraged me daily. I knew this road would be a long road ahead. I was misunderstood by many, and I felt my pastor and first lady didn't understand me. I'm so grateful they never gave up on me and that they were there for me. My healing began. I gained my reconnection with God. I started not only reading my Word, but I started speaking God's Word to myself. John 10:10 states, "The thief comes only but to kill, steal, and destroy, but I am come that you might have life more abundantly." I spoke this daily. Philippians 4:13 states, "I can do all things through Christ that strengthen me." I didn't just read it, I believed it. Romans 8:3 states, "Yet in all these things we are more than conquerors through Him that loves us."

I started to feel God's presence again. I felt the love He had for me. I went back to the church and started fellowshipping with God's people again. I repented to God. I asked Him to forgive me and heal my backsliding. God started to overflow me with blessings. Step by step and day by day, God would bless me. God gave me the strength to do for me what I couldn't do. He poured out His amazing grace in my life.

I began to catch my breath. I forgave the people who'd mistreated and misused me. I had to forgive my daddy for sexually assaulting me. Ultimately, I had to forgive myself for letting life overtake me.

God blessed me with a job. I got my driver's license and a car. God did it for me. Now I was breathing in and out; I was walking in God's blessings. I was finally free in my heart and in my spirit. I had to regroup. I had to let go of certain things that got in the way of my relationship with God. I had to make some very hard decisions, but for me to keep breathing, I had to keep the enemy out of my life. Every decision I made, I had to put God first. Matthew 19:26 states, "But Jesus looked at them and said to them, with man this is impossible but with God all things are possible."

Now I know, by God's grace, it's possible to live that abundant life. God is a second chance God. It gave me another chance to get it right. People may give up on you, but God is faithful. Joshua 1:5 states, "No man shall be able to stand before you all the days of your life: as I was with Moses, so shall I be with you. I will never leave thee nor forsake thee." I got my joy back, I got my peace back, and I got my life back. There is no looking back. I cannot doubt Him because I know too much about Him. He has proven to be God in my life. For God I live or for God I die. I overcame all the impossible by God's grace.

BREATHE
An Anthology Compiled by Melinda Walker

Demetre Francis

Demetre Francis is thirty-one years old. She has an eight-year-old daughter named Arie'l Armstrong whom she loves with all her heart. She has a saying that it's her, Arie'l, and God. She was born and raised in Prentis, Mississippi.

At the age of eighteen, Demetre joined the Outreach Fellowship Revival Center, where she was saved and taught the Word of God under the leadership of Pastor Jessie Holloway and the late Barbara Jean Holloway. Throughout many difficult and trying times, she was inspired to write in this anthology as a co-author. She wants to inspire others to face every obstacle in life leaning on Jesus. There is nothing impossible with God. She is a prayer warrior who believes prayer changes things. She has been called to intercede and stand in the gap for her family. She also leads prayer services on some Sundays during morning call outs.

Demetre is not a person who has to be out front. She fights her battles on her knees. Many days she comes to the church alone just to pray and seek God's face. Her heart is for the hurting. Prayer is what she has been called to do, and she uses that weapon for the warfare she faces daily in her life. She stands on the promises of God.

"Ask and keep on asking, seek and keep on seeking, knock and keeping on knocking, and it will be given to me, I shall find and the doors will be open unto me."

Contact Demetre at:

francisdemetre@yahoo.com
demetre.francis.75.facebook.com

www.ingramcontent.com/pod-product-compliance
Lightning Source LLC
Chambersburg PA
CBHW032130090426
42743CB00007B/549